SACRED SILENCE

DONALD COZZENS

SACRED SILENCE

Denial and the Crisis
in the Church

LITURGICAL PRESS
Collegeville, Minnesota

www.litpress.org

Cover design by Ann Blattner.

1   2   3   4   5   6   7   8

Library of Congress Cataloging-in-Publication Data

Cozzens, Donald B.
   Sacred silence : denial and the crisis in the church / Donald Cozzens.
      199 p. ; 24 cm.
   Includes bibliographical references (p. 173–192) and index.
   ISBN 0-8146-2779-X — ISBN 0-8146-2731-5 (pbk.)
   1. Child sexual abuse by clergy. 2. Catholic Church—Clergy—Sexual
behavior.   I. Title.

BX1912.9.C69   2002
282'.09'0511—dc21   2002016146

In memory of Bishops
P. Francis Murphy
and Raymond A. Lucker.

Men of faith and courage
who dared to break the silence.

CONTENTS

Acknowledgments   1

Introduction   5

Part One: Masks of Denial

Chapter One: Sacred Silence   11

Chapter Two: Forms of Denial   26

Part Two: Faces of Denial

Chapter Three: Sacred Oaths, Sacred Promises   37

Chapter Four: Voices of Women   49

Chapter Five: Religious Life and the Priesthood   65

Chapter Six: Abuse of Our Children   89

Chapter Seven: Clerical Culture   112

Chapter Eight: Gay Men in the Priesthood   124

Chapter Nine: Ministry and Leadership   140

Part Three: Beyond Denial

Chapter Ten: Sacred Silence, Sacred Speech   157

Notes   173

Index   193

ACKNOWLEDGMENTS

THE DUST JACKET OF THIS BOOK, a photograph through a medieval arched window, was taken by my friend and teacher, Kilian Hufgard, O.S.U. A master artist skilled in a number of mediums, Sister Kilian formerly taught art and the history of art at Ursuline College in Pepper Pike, Ohio, where I met her while teaching at the same college in the 1980s. I was surprised and honored when this distinguished professor *emerita* audited a number of my classes in religious studies and psychology and further honored when she agreed to tutor me in her theory of art and architecture—with emphasis on the contribution of Bernard of Clairvaux, about whom she had written with passion and insight. During these almost weekly afternoon meetings in her studio, I felt like one of the disciples on the road to Emmaus as Sister Kilian explained, better revealed, the convergence of philosophical insight, the Christian life, and the creative process. Her synthesis—and her simple yet profound authenticity—awakened my imagination and expanded my soul. How does one say thank you for such a gift?

Here was a scholar of the first order, an artist whose work was always praise, a poet who honored the words she wove into songs of wonder and gratitude. From this good and wise woman I discovered that truth and beauty emerge from goodness—from that which is real and from that which is well made. For Sister Kilian, the real, as distinct from the synthetic and from all that is display, was the ground of God's revelation. The good and the real she believed with passion, were the true markers of the divine. There was no higher praise for an artifact or a work of art than for Sister Kilian to speak of it as good, real (honest), and useful. The spirit of Kilian Hufgard has influenced the pages that follow. My hope is that she will find this book real (honest)—and good.

I also wish to acknowledge with gratitude my former teacher and long-time friend, Thomas O'Meara, O.P., who has just completed a twenty-two year tenure in the theology department at the University of Notre Dame. From Tom I learned that a teacher does not want the student to exclaim only "I know" but also "I see."

The following friends and colleagues read this book in manuscript and improved it immensely with their comments, corrections, and suggestions. I express my sincere gratitude to Colette Ackerman, O.C.D., Patrick Henry, Mary Catherine Hilkert, O.P., Robert Toth, and Stephanie Weisgram, O.S.B.

St. John's University, tucked into the rolling hills of central Minnesota, is home to the Institute for Ecumenical and Cultural Research. Established in 1967 by the renowned ecumenist and theologian, Kilian McDonnell, O.S.B., the Institute provides an ideal place for writers on sabbatical. It was here that I wrote *Sacred Silence* as part of an ecumenical community of resident scholars. My colleagues regularly made important contributions to my writing by suggesting relevant books and articles, some quite central to my topic. This book is stronger because of them. I am grateful to E. Byron Anderson, Charles Bouchard, O.P., Cathy Campbell, Daniel Grigassy, O.F.M., Donald Klinefelter, Reid Locklin, Sharon McMillan, S.N.D. de N., Mary Margaret Pazdan, O.P., Ernest Ranly, C.PP.S., and Sharon Reives.

The Institute's executive director, Patrick Henry, executive associate, Dolores Schuh, C.H.M., liaison officer Wilfred Theisen, O.S.B., Stephanie Hart, student intern, and Kilian McDonnell, O.S.B., became good friends. I treasure our spirited conversations about matters both sacred and secular.

A number of the St. John's University and College of St. Benedict community hosted memorable evenings of gracious dining and engaging conversation—Rose and Peter Dwyer, Kathleen Cahalan, College of St. Benedict president Mary Lyons, Linda Maloney, Sarah Pruett and John Merkle, Judith and Mark Twomey, and Susan Wood, S.C.L. Conversations with these colleagues honed and strengthened the present volume. I am also grateful to the Benedictine sisters of St. Joseph, Minnesota, for the wit and warmth of memorable conversations.

The staff of the Alcuin Library at St. John's University offered generous and timely research assistance in the writing of this book for which I thank them sincerely.

I also wish to thank the staff of The Liturgical Press, whose offices are located, to my good fortune, on the St. John's University campus. Peter Dwyer, Mark Twomey, Joe Riley, Colleen Stiller, Ann Blattner, and Ken Brokamp played key roles in the development and production of *Sacred Silence.*

For the final editing phase of this book, Murlan Jeremiah Murphy offered comfortable lodging and quiet space to see this project to completion. I am grateful for his friendship and hospitality.

Finally, I want to express my gratitude to Cleveland Bishop Anthony Pilla for granting me sabbatical leave and for releasing me from diocesan assignment so that I might return to college teaching.

Donald Bernard Cozzens

Feast of Pentecost
May 19, 2002
Collegeville, Minnesota

INTRODUCTION

"WHAT ARE WE AFRAID OF?"

The question was put to me by a U.S. archbishop. It was, of course, rhetorical. He knew we Christians really have nothing to be afraid of if we place our faith and hope in the gospel, in the promise of Jesus Christ to be with his disciples to the end of time. On another level, the question is anything but rhetorical. There appears to be a great deal that many Christians, and especially church leaders, are quite literally afraid of. This book is an attempt to answer the question, "What are we afraid of?" and to address the deeper questions, "Why are we afraid?" "Why is the institutional church so defensive?" "Why is it so controlling?" How is it that a church that is the bearer of the Word and the champion of the oppressed can maintain unholy silences while denying that obvious pastoral and ecclesial problems, indeed crises, even exist?

"We are, in church and in society, in big trouble," writes the renowned scripture scholar, Walter Brueggemann.[1] Few, if any, would question his judgment. In the pages that follow we will examine some of the issues and concerns that are both symptoms and causes of the present crisis—and especially the denial, itself a symptom and a cause—which exacerbates the church's "big trouble." (References that follow to the "church," unless otherwise noted, will be to the Roman Catholic Church.)

The focus of the church's troubles in spring 2002 was first and foremost on the ever-expanding clergy sexual abuse scandal. In a number of ways it is unlike previous sex scandals involving priests, religious, and bishops. For one thing, it is unmasking a systemic or structural crisis that threatens the current lines of power that have gone unchallenged for centuries. This in itself is enough to make some prelates and clergy afraid, very afraid. Another is the Catholic anger rising from conservatives, moderates, and progressives alike against the duplicitous arrogance of some prominent archbishops and other church authorities. While angry with priest pederasts, Catholics are especially angry with bishops who have placed the resources of the church and the reputation of the priesthood ahead of the safety of children and teenagers. Added to the repressed anger large numbers of Catholics have been nursing since the publication of Pope Paul VI's anti-birth control encyclical in 1968 and the unrealized promise of the Second Vatican Council, the current rage is galvanizing the laity into a force to be reckoned with.

The laity, moreover, sense what many church authorities are reluctant to acknowledge—that the present troubles go well beyond the priest abuse debacle. Underneath the mushrooming scandals and the painful polarization shaking the confidence of the faithful, a church stands at the brink of destabilization. How could it be otherwise? A still feudal church struggles to meet the modern world as the modern world merges with post-modern currents of thought that threaten religious belief as we know it. We may not have reason to be afraid, but we have abundant reason to be anxious. And as history makes clear, where anxiety dwells, imagination shrivels, denial thrives, and control becomes obsessive. An anxious church bureaucracy displays precisely these characteristics—denial, legalism, controlling power, secrecy.

The abuse scandals of the past twenty years or so have served as the "tipping point" for a new era of Catholic life. What that life will look like will be determined in the years ahead. The thesis of *Sacred Silence* is that our first challenge is to break through the wall of denial and silence guarding the present ecclesial order. I argue in the pages ahead that we are in need of a brave, "redemptive honesty" if we are to move in the direction of a healthier, holier church.[2]

In the meantime, both the church and its priesthood are in virtual exile—displaced in our own homes, rectories, and chanceries. We feel the winds of discontent while we stumble tentatively in one direction and then in another, disoriented and discouraged. We know in our bones the present trouble is like no other. We also believe, like our Jewish ancestors in exile centuries ago, that God is with us and that our exile "in place" is pregnant with insight and deliverance. In exile, where confusion eclipses clarity and once secure identities are blurred, we are thrown back on our spiritual foundations, on our understanding of what matters most. In this land of dislocation we remember that without faith and hope—and honesty—we are lost. As exiles we come to see that we are in the midst of a profound ecclesial transition which demands struggle against old mental habits and institutional inertia if we are to emerge a renewed and vital church. Walter Brueggemann captures the hope and potential of the exile experience:

> [T]he *traditions of exile* in the Old Testament—remarkably rich, generative, and imaginative—might be a source and indeed perhaps the only resource of speech and imagination that can move us *under denial to reality* and beyond *despair into possibility* (emphasis in the original). Ancient Israel understood that unless the loss is processed in order to penetrate the denial and despair, newness will not come. It is not, I suspect, different among us.[3]

Here in exile, then, in this time of passage, we find a fertile place for reflection, imagination, and speech. We find a place where we might move from denial to reality, from despair to possibility. This implies, however, serious soul-work. Perhaps our first step is to grieve all that was good and holy in the old order now passing away, for there is no spiritual depth where individuals and communities do not grieve their losses. Many of us are not good at grieving; we feel it means dwelling in pain or sorrow. To a certain extent, of course, we do give space to our pain, to our losses, but that is only right and necessary. Only after honest grieving can we see the horizon of promise and deliverance.

If Brueggemann is correct, an awakened imagination emerges from authentic grieving which in turn leads to honest speech. With fresh eyes and liberated hearts, people in exile learn how to speak and to "tell the truth in love."[4]

Finally, a word about the word "sacred." Clearly it denotes a silence emanating from a religious source, in this case, the church. I intend, however, to capture the rich ambiguity of the term. The Latin *sacer* is sometimes translated "sacred" and sometimes "accursed." Understood in its broadest sense,

> The sacred consists of all those forces whose dominance over man [sic] increases or seems to increase in proportion to man's effort to master them. Tempests, forest fires, and plagues, among other phenomena, may be classified as sacred.[5]

What we cannot control, therefore, may be understood as sacred—sunrises and sunsets, tidal waves, falling in love, cancer, unearned loyalty. Also, that which is beyond us: the divine, the numinous, the mysterious, are referenced as sacred. On clear summer nights, children and the child-like stand in awe, humility, and gratitude looking up at the distant stars. They gaze in sacred silence.

Historian and philosopher Rene Girard, moreover, insists that violence and the sacred are one and the same thing.[6] The scapegoat as sacrificial victim, for example, is separated from the tribe—placed beyond the tribe—in order to be killed for the "welfare of the group." Both the victim and the sacrificial act become "sacred." From this Girardian perspective we may perceive silence and denial in the church as the antithesis of the more common understanding of sacred—as forms of violence perpetrated by religious authorities for "the good of the church." Or, more honestly, for the preservation of clerical structures that serve their own interests.

For too long now, an unholy silence and an unhealthy denial have held sway. Catholics now see this sad reality and they are convinced it simply cannot continue. They are ready to assume their rightful responsibility, in partnership with their ordained brothers, to serve the church they love. As if in exile, the faithful yearn for words of honesty, hope, and direction. In this time of peril and promise, *Sacred Silence* extends an invitation: Let the conversation begin.

PART ONE

MASKS OF DENIAL

CHAPTER ONE

SACRED SILENCE

They are afraid of offending and making enemies—and all of this because of self-love. Sometimes it's just that they would like to keep peace, and this, I tell you, is the worst cruelty one can inflict. If a sore is not cauterized or excised when necessary, but only ointment is applied, not only will it not heal, but it will infect the whole [body], often fatally . . . .

—Catherine of Siena, Doctor of the Church,
from a letter to Pope Gregory XI

There is no spiritual life which does not encounter deception and disillusionment, suffering and confusion.

—Jean Sulivan, *Morning Light*

THE SILENCE, DENIAL, AND MINIMIZATION discussed in these pages have numerous roots—some conscious, others unconscious, some personal, others more properly associated with the collective mindset that binds a people as believers. Exploring these roots may allow us to see what is it that keeps so many alert and intelligent people of faith from addressing with candor and courage the issues and challenges that weigh heavy on our church at the beginning of the twenty-first century.

The present phenomenon of denial and minimization, which I term for shorthand purposes, silence, can be found in every century of the church's long history. It clearly is part and parcel of the human condition—a human condition whose myths of origin relate startling examples of denial and rationalization. The pattern of refusing to see, of refusing to acknowledge symptoms and signs that beg for attention, study, and reflection has led to many of history's great blunders.[1] It also has led us to scratch our heads at the puzzling human behaviors that wound, often tragically, personal, family, and societal relationships.

Each of our own stories, of course, each of our spiritual journeys is shaped and directed by defining moments of deception and rationalization. Often occasions for insight and even wisdom, they nonetheless mark those moments when the light seemed unbearable, when we could do no better than pretend that all was well. No doubt the root cause of our personal and collective denial and minimization, of our less than sacred silence, can be traced to the great and enduring wound we name *original sin.*[2]

Along the way, we have learned that silence postpones conflict and tension and seems to ease the simmering anxiety that floats just below our conscious comings and goings. In our hearts we believe that truth will set us free, indeed, truth will be our salvation. Yet every age, every culture, every religion, provides a shaded lens that allows us to live a lie, to hear without listening, to speak without love.

What we examine here is not new. It echoes the follies of ages past. It is, however, timely. Our present resistance to issues and concerns relating to the church in general and ministry in particular is in need of analysis and study. The immediate vitality of our church is at stake and her mission remains endangered if we choose to maintain this sacred silence.

Three themes appear central to our examination of the roots of our present malaise—loyalty, responsibility, and tranquility. Each in turn will be considered here.

Loyalty

Personal experience as well as our collective memory make it clear that to speak the truth as one sees it, no matter that it is spoken "in love," runs the risk of being perceived as disloyal.[3] Certain practices, structures, customs, and beliefs, even if they are clearly open to historical development, are judged by the controlling polity as too dangerous to address. To nonetheless speak one's truth, even the simple call for discussion of neuralgic issues invites the charge of disloyalty. And when the verdict of disloyalty is passed, the subject under judgment experiences some degree of psychological and social isolation. The human need for being *a part of*, for belonging, for the respect of one's peers is threatened. A certain suffering of soul is inevitable.

Why, we may ask, do faith-based institutions such as the church, which we now understand to be in need of ongoing renewal and even reform, respond with inertia and resistance when called upon to examine current structures and practices? Often, as we shall see, this resistance is sustained by a misguided sense of loyalty. Over the years, even centuries, historically conditioned practices, customs, and teachings take on the dignity of divinely revealed dogmas. The mere suggestion that they be reviewed in the light of changing times and pastoral experience is determined by some members of the church, especially some of its leaders, to be dangerous, and those calling for such reviews disloyal.

In the eyes of many leaders and members of the church—and here I speak principally of the Latin rite of the Roman Catholic Church—her enemies are seen as numerous, deceitful, and ready to exploit any real or perceived flaw or weakness. To call attention to areas in need of possible structural reform, therefore, such as mandated celibacy or the ordination of married individuals, is seen by such leaders and members of the church as disloyal. The message is clear. The church, still considered by some to be a "perfect society," does not welcome calls for discussion or review of customs or practices that have proven useful and even noble in times past.

The message is sometimes made explicit, e.g., "The Holy Father or the diocesan bishop does not want discussion about this or that issue." More often than not, clergy and laity sense their bishop's discomfort when certain issues or practices are raised. Where this is the case, I suspect that a bishop's understanding of loyalty to the church is at the heart of his discomfort. He doesn't even want to come close to situations that may be interpreted by his priests or people as not in complete harmony with the current discipline or practice of the church. When this is the case, not only are important questions and concerns left unaddressed, the spirit and morale of priests, religious, and laity are undermined. The need for control behind this kind of unspoken message tends to shrink the souls of those who perceive it. As The Dogmatic Constitution on Church affirms, competent adults have an obligation to speak about their concerns to church leaders.[4] To do anything less is to ignore one's responsibility as an adult member of the faithful. Silence of this sort is disingenuous. In spite of this clear moral obligation to speak one's truth in love, to speak from one's experience and reflection respectfully yet forthrightly, even in closed ecclesial settings such as convocations of priests or meetings of diocesan pastoral councils, requires considerable moral courage.

I argue here that it is a sense of loyalty to the gospel and to the institutional church that often prompts the breaking of an unholy silence, that brings a man or woman to speak respectfully and directly to church authorities and others about what matters to them most. It is a sense of loyalty that prompts members of the faithful—laity, religious, priests, and bishops—to call for discussion of issues that may indeed be dangerous to face but ultimately will be more dangerous to the church if not faced.

Our history records numerous cases of "disloyal-loyalty," of men and women of faith raising issues that seemed to be out of bounds. Paul speaks directly to Peter concerning the application of Jewish laws and customs relative to Gentile converts; Bernard of Clairvaux and Catherine of Siena speak their truth boldly "in love" to popes, princes, and bishops; Teresa of Avila and Joan of Arc, from centuries past, Yves Congar, Cardinal Suenens, and John Courtney Murray in more recent times, spoke the truth as they understood it out of loyalty to the gospel and church.

Copernicus and Galileo trusted their understanding of scientific truth to the peril of their very lives. Their personal conviction to what they held to be scientifically true caused them to be judged not only disloyal to the church, but heretical at the time when heresy often led to torture and death. These great minds would have smiled, I believe, at the observation of Karl Ernst von Baer, the nineteenth-century founder of modern embryology, who remarked that all new and truly important ideas must pass through three stages: first dismissed as nonsense, then rejected as against religion, and finally acknowledged as true, with the proviso from initial opponents that they knew it all along.[5]

The silence of which we speak, however, is not so much directed against new and important ideas, but against the modest call for open and respectful attention to issues profoundly affecting the spiritual lives of today's Catholics. Church authorities to whom the call is made display authentic loyalty to the gospel and to the spirit of Vatican II when they listen with open minds and hearts to the concerns of believers shaped by their pastoral experience and their love of their Christian faith. Beyond loyalty to the gospel and the tradition of the church, such nondefensive listening is simply their duty.

Responsibility

Few modern Catholics doubt that bishops bear particularly heavy burdens in today's post-conciliar church. Not the least of these burdens is the responsibility to keep the faithful of their diocese in communion with each other and their diocese in communion with the universal church under the unifying ministry of the bishop of Rome. One can easily imagine the weight of this responsibility in an age marked by declining numbers of candidates for the priesthood, an expanding Catholic population, aging clergy and religious, and well-educated laity seeking compelling reasons to support the pronouncements they hear from their bishops and pastoral leaders.[6] These and other realities facing the church at the beginning of the twenty-first century have made episcopal leadership an especially difficult and challenging ministry.

Added to their burden is the perception of some Catholics that bishops who are not open to discussion about controversial and potentially divisive issues are jealously guarding their power. They are accused of being more concerned about their authority and other issues of control than of leading their people to a deeper experience of the freedom and light of the gospel. Without question, there are bishops who delight in the controlling exercise of episcopal power. For these bishops, the exercise of authority provides an exhilarating sense of vitality and power. If we concede that power, in a certain sense, is intoxicating, dulling the anxieties of our human finitude and isolation, it can easily become the cornerstone of an individual's identity.[7] In our culture, individuals with power are *somebodies*. Should this dynamic work its way into the psyche of a bishop, it is likely that he will feel no real desire to listen to either his priests or the people of his local church. He is *the* teacher, after all, let others listen.

I believe this is the case with a relatively small number of bishops. Most bishops, I am convinced, are not at all covetous of more and more power, of greater and greater control. And I think they are genuinely perplexed when they hear of conversations suggesting that their main concern is the maintenance or expansion of their authority and power. As the writer Raymond Hedin has observed, "[M]ost men inside a hierarchical system feel much more powerless than those who are even more powerless realize—than women, that is, in the case of the church and many other systems."[8] Still, sometimes just below the level of conscious reflection, positions of power and social status with their accompanying titles shore up one's sense of being. The sense of limitation and inherent anxiety that are part and parcel of the human condition are numbed—as with a shot of novocaine—and the concomitant feelings of preferment, of being chosen, of being special all contribute to a habit of mind that makes honest communication difficult. Here the unconscious dynamics of power are often at play prompting, on a conscious level, patterns of perception that others easily see as forms of denial and minimization.

Not only has the system worked for these individuals in terms of prestige and status, it has worked to assuage the anxiety so inseparably linked to human finitude. Of course, the soothing effect of power and status on existential anxiety needs constant reinforcement. Like the numbing effect of novocaine, it wears off unless one's sense of power and status remains clear and unchallenged. For Christians, and especially for Christian leaders, i.e., bishops and priests, the courage to face existential anxiety and to transcend it is found precisely in the self-gift modeled in the self-surrender of Jesus Christ. Authentic discipleship, which is always grounded in the power of the Spirit, subverts the power dynamics manifested in fearful and controlling leaders. And it breaks the grip of denial, minimization, and secrecy.[9]

When such habits of mind and psyche are joined in church leaders who cling to nonhistorical understandings of theology and church teaching, the result is a tenacious defense of the way things are. Examples of such habits of mind and psyche abound. Church authorities, to name but one, felt the very authority of the Bible was at stake when Galileo announced his revolutionary discovery. Convinced that it was their responsibility to defend the authority of the Scriptures, they denied the scientific evidence before them. With this mentality, the way things are, is the way things must be. Open discussion of issues and patterns that bear directly on the faith life of believers, that might lead to structural or systemic change, threatens the very spiritual and psychic world that gives meaning and purpose to their lives. Denial and silence inevitably follow.

But like the misguided sense of loyalty discussed above, there is a misguided sense of responsibility. It can be observed in the bishop who believes it is his responsibility to listen defensively to every proposal for dialogue or change in church discipline that comes to him. It can be seen in the bishop who welcomes dialogue, but listens only to answer questions or to point out the difficulties of a given proposal. Bishops, like the rest of us, need to be shaped and formed by their sisters and brothers in Christ—by the laity, by their brother bishops, and by the religious, deacons, and priests

with whom they live and work. This requires of them a fundamental trust in the men and women who make up the local
church, in those who come forward to speak out of their experience as Christians struggling to lead gospel-based lives, and, especially, in their priests and the pastoral ministers who staff the
parishes and offices of their diocese. And it requires a commitment
to sustain effective communication, effective channels for the
open exchange of ideas. Where this is the case, the vitality and
health of the local church energizes both the diocesan bishop and
the pastoral leaders of the diocese.

Precisely, then, because he is shepherd and leader of the local
church, a bishop has the responsibility to listen from the heart to
the concerns of his people and pastoral leaders. Bishops who display
this kind of openness and trust stay focused on their mission—to
bring the light and freedom of the gospel to our world. They
understand that they are to be, *par excellence,* men of the Word
who are responsible for bringing the saving power of the Word of
God to their local church and beyond. Their responsibility to
church unity and order, to their brother bishops and the bishop of
Rome, is only enhanced when they confront tendencies to deny or
minimize the disturbing and challenging issues of the day.

Tranquility

In spring 2000, amidst the controversy that followed in the
wake of my book *The Changing Face of the Priesthood,* a bishop
who, in my judgment, enjoys a particularly astute understanding
of the temperaments of U.S. bishops remarked to me that he believed most bishops accepted the reality of the issues I raised.[10]
They understood, furthermore, that these issues needed to be addressed. They simply didn't want to address them, he said, "on
their watch." The bishop's remark struck a chord.

To the extent that his read is accurate—I believe it hits the
mark in more than a few cases—it points to a striking failure of
leadership. It also sheds light on the phenomenon of denial and

minimization with which many church leaders greet reports of concern and crisis relating to the affairs of their local church and, especially, to the priesthood and ministry. Addressing them, they understand, would surface considerable conflict and might well shatter the tranquility, at least the surface tranquility, of their diocese. When our analysis takes into account the concern bishops have that their people may be confused or scandalized by an open and nondefensive approach to the issues I raised in *The Changing Face of the Priesthood*, our anatomy of denial offers, I trust, some understanding of the dynamics behind the current sacred silence.

When the desire for comfort and calm matter too much in an individual's life, the spirit of adventure and the possibility of real achievement are sacrificed. Even tranquility has its shadow side. Consider the wisdom of President John Adams' wife, Abigail, writing to her son, John Quincy, as he is about to accompany his father on a perilous journey to France:

> It is not in the still calm of life, or the repose of a pacific station, that great characters are formed. The habits of a vigorous mind are formed in contending with difficulties. Great necessities call out great virtues. When a mind is raised, and animated by scenes that engage the heart, then those qualities which would otherwise lay dormant, wake into life and form the character of the hero and the statesman.[11]

Church leaders, bishops in particular, take on, in a sense, the roles of statesmen and patriots. They ought to seek those habits of the heart common to statesmen and patriots—wisdom, prudence, and courage. Nothing less will do in this post-conciliar period of the church. True leaders of every age have shown themselves to be women and men of great heart. They have always been thoughtful, open-minded, and without fear. Many were saints. All, in my judgment, were heroes.

Underneath the desire for tranquility and the avoidance of conflict, I suspect, are fears and anxieties that are not always conscious. If the veil of denial is lifted, the issues revealed will require resolve and most likely some form of action. And the action called for will in turn bring about change. Significant change, we know, is seldom met without considerable fear and anxiety. The personal and institutional discomfort resulting from the mere anticipation of facing and dealing with difficult issues tends to reinforce the denial. Under the guise of prudence and discretion, disingenuous questions are raised: Just where might honest discussion and open dialogue take us? Perhaps this is not the right time to address such complex issues? Fear of being required to make difficult decisions and the fear of having to take timely action can immobilize even the most committed church leaders. The understandable fear, I propose, should be considered with compassion, even though it is difficult to square with a life of deep faith. Failing to draw on the Spirit of God for the courage to lead in the face of fear is another matter.

Finally, from the point of view of the diocesan bishop, raising the curtain of denial and minimization will likely invite criticism from at least some of his brother bishops—a source of some anxiety for any individual who understandably seeks the affirmation of his or her peers. The situation becomes especially acute for the bishop eager to move on to a more attractive or influential diocese.

Official Truth

Echoing Pontius Pilate's cynical question, though often without the cynicism, people of faith in every period of the church's history implicitly ask: "What is truth?" And sincere men and women continue to ask: "What is the right thing to do in this particular situation?" "What, in fact, does the Gospel require of me here and now?" For many believers, the answer that cuts through the ambiguities and complexities of institutional life, the anxieties awakened when personal experience is in tension with traditional church teaching, and the ongoing struggle for integrity and moral rectitude, is to turn to the "official truth" proclaimed by Vatican offices and papal pronouncements. There is wisdom in this turn. For wisdom and truth are indeed found, if not in every pronouncement, in what we term here "official truth." We especially reverence and embrace those teachings of the church that our tradition holds up as dogma, as divinely revealed.

But official truth, as I use the term here, also includes a broad spectrum of teachings, traditions, practices, disciplines, and customs that fall outside the rubric of divine revelation. These are the factors and variables, if you will, that give form to Catholic culture. While not dogmatic in nature, they nonetheless shape and determine the everyday lives of believers. To the extent that they are grounded in gospel values and the best tradition of the church, they will support, counsel, and encourage the laity, religious, and clergy in their efforts to live fully the new life they possess in Jesus Christ. These nondogmatic truths themselves have been shaped and refined by the varied experiences of men and women living the Christian life. They remain normative, I propose, under the validation of authentic human experience.

Whenever human experience, supported by theological and pastoral reflection, stands in contrast to these teachings and practices, however, they require serious discussion and review. But the very nature of institutional life, as we shall see shortly, seems to resist this kind of process. Without fail there will be various levels of fear, anxiety, and tension. Vested interests will be put at risk and comfortable lifestyles will be threatened. When this is the case, defensive attitudes are assumed and the issue at hand is framed in such a manner that individuals feel reluctant to pursue it. Pressure is felt to embrace the "official truth" that may denigrate and devalue the "personal truth" of committed Christians who see a clear need for open discussion and discernment guided by the Spirit.[12] Voices of experience are not heard, or if heard, not taken seriously. Silence follows and denial spreads.

What is needed, I believe, is to understand that official truth stands in dialectical tension with "common truth" grounded in the experience of faithful believers striving to live in right relationship with God, each other, and all of creation. We now believe that the Spirit of God has enlightened both truths. Ultimately, of course, the truths of our dialectical poles are one truth, just as the two ends of a pencil have their own identity due to their participation in the reality of the one and same pencil. The dialectical poles under discussion, here, are really two faces of the same reality. Both, in respectful tension and harmonious communion, make it possible for the pilgrim people of God to discover what God has revealed and what God continues to reveal through the abiding presence of the Spirit. While we as church readily acknowledge the value of human experience, we continue to listen to its many and varied voices with considerable mistrust. The more is the pity. For the credibility of both "truths" is enhanced when each receives the reverence it deserves.

Institutional Dynamics

Elsewhere I discussed the research of psychologists and other social scientists on the effects of denial in the corporate world.[13] Large, successful corporations, the research showed, exhibit the same tendencies to denial and minimization that can be found in rectories, chanceries, and Vatican offices. Sustained growth, financial strength, and stock splits all contributed to a common mentality among the companies' officers which consistently proved to be insular and elitist. Apparently, their shrewd planning and proven track record lulled them into a state of confidence and triumphalism, which in turn made them less open to ideas and proposals that seemed in conflict with the structures, strategies, and policies that generated such overall success and wide margins of profit. Corporate officials became wary of managers reporting data that indicated the need for significant changes or new directions. They became less and less interested in the opinions and suggestions of their middle managers who were increasingly seen as employees whose main responsibility was to implement the directives of the upper echelon executives.

Such attitudes of senior executives fostered, in turn, a culture of denial. Data of all sorts—marketing reports, trends in foreign sectors, and the like—were not given the weight they deserved.

Ultimately this failure in leadership set the stage for staggering reverses.[14]

Growing up in Argentina's political and social chaos of the 1970s, business consultant Fred Kofman describes the culture of denial that settled on most of its citizens. "We were all assuming that things were fine—and they were, on the surface—and yet we all knew that the country was very ill at the core." People, he notes, wanted to believe that as long as things looked more or less normal on the surface, they could carry on with their lives:

> For a while that worked and the society was operating normally while, at the same time, there were concentration camps, people being tortured and murdered, right in our midst. I was only 14 years old at the time, and it was very disturbing to me because I felt something was wrong, and yet I didn't know what it was. I developed this tremendous distaste for situations where everything seems fine on the surface, and yet people are suffering underneath. And I associate this state with denial. . . ."[15]

Years later while working as a consultant with various corporations, Kofman discovered a striking similarity to the culture of denial he first knew as a boy in Argentina. While the realities being denied were drastically different, what mattered was putting a tranquil face on interactions with colleagues and superiors, a face that obscured the real issues calling for attention. I was reminded of parish and diocesan staff meetings when I read Kofman's account of a business meeting he had attended:

> [P]eople apparently were having a normal meeting—not particularly productive, but I wouldn't say horrible—and yet I was feeling the same way I was feeling in Argentina. And then after interviewing the people out of the meeting or hearing them speak about what had happened, I realized that the meeting was a farce. But it was worse than that. It was that they *knew* it was a farce—everybody knew. So it was the same kind of craziness—not physical violence, but people were participating in a charade where everybody knew they were not telling the truth and that others were not telling the

truth and they were not talking about the real issues. Everybody knew this but nobody wanted to say that the emperor had no clothes.[16]

Pastoral leaders and church personnel are not business persons, of course, but they have no less a need to be honest about what is really going on, about the challenges confronting the church and its mission. Far too many Vatican, diocesan, and parish staff meetings, I suspect, conclude with the truth left untold and the real issues judged too risky to raise. Better to tolerate the subtle encroachments on one's integrity than to risk upsetting the powers that be. The vague feeling of guilt and unrest that often accompany the participants as they rise from the table sooner or later begins to fade. They get on with their work, and the culture of denial is reinforced.

Kofman and others remind us that the church, as a human institution, remains subject to the dynamics common to other organizations and institutions. It will be argued, of course, that the church is not the kind of institution that can be compared to the corporate giants of commerce and industry. Without question, there are significant differences. The church, after all, has a divine commission to bring the light and freedom of the gospel to the entire human family. And it has its own astounding track record. Still, I argue here that the flourishing that followed the church's humble beginning, the survival of persecution after persecution, the unity and communion sustained by the abiding presence of the Spirit, these and so many other manifestations of grace, do not negate the human, social, and institutional dynamics we have just examined. Its shepherds and pastors, its curial officials and chancery staffers, for the most part individuals of considerable talent and commitment, experience the same pressures, both internal and external, conscious and unconscious, to stay the course taken by their predecessors as their corporate counterparts. It should not surprise us, then, that church leaders tend to be conservative, cautious, and guarded. It is simply the nature of things.

While I concede the inevitable institutional instincts that support a culture of denial and mistrust, I believe it is a manifestation of the church that is far from its best. The church is indeed susceptible to human folly and sin, but it is also the sacrament of Jesus Christ, informed and inspired by the Spirit to reveal the abiding love of the God who remains ultimate mystery. As such, it is a beacon of hope and a promise of salvation for each and every age and culture it encounters. It professes to bear a "word from the Lord," a message of salvation for God's people enfleshed in the person of Jesus of Nazareth whom we now confess as the Christ. It is a pilgrim people who walk by the light of the Spirit of God sustained by word and sacrament. When we as church walk by faith, we have the power to transcend our human tendency to put fear ahead of trust and caution ahead of courage.

Fear, of course, is neither a moral act nor an omission. Uninvited, it wells up in the human heart. But cowardice is. Whenever we employ denial and silence out of fear and anxiety, we sin against faith. The very institutional postures we assume to guard our faith, expose our lack of faith.

As we shall see in the chapters ahead, what really scandalizes countless numbers of the faithful is the church's readiness—tragically exemplified in recent decades by its response to the sexual misconduct cases involving a significant number of priests and bishops—to deny and minimize the depth, scope, and pastoral implications of issues that cry out for analysis and action.

CHAPTER TWO

FORMS OF DENIAL

Each of us is aware in ourselves of the workings of denial, of our need to be innocent of a troubling recognition.

—Christopher Bollas, *Being a Character*

We've all gotten to be experts at not facing things.

—Fr. Francis Mulcahy, M*A*S*H*

BEFORE TURNING TO THE FACES OF DENIAL operative in the church today, it is helpful to examine the more prevalent forms denial assumes in ecclesial and social circles. The focus, for the most part, will be on institutional patterns of denial, but such is the human proneness to self-deception and denial, that ordinary believers, not only church leaders, will likely find themselves in the following categories.

While denial and minimization are common and understandable human foibles evident in mischievous children seeking to avoid parental disciplining as well as adults defending themselves against embarrassing mistakes or scandalous behaviors threatening loss of face or more serious consequences, they unmask a fundamental inclination to defend one's sense of self-worth or corporate-worth with often torturous bendings and twistings of reality. The conventional wisdom that denial often makes bad situations worse holds little currency when individuals or institutions are threatened and the dynamics of denial kick in. The temptation to deny and minimize, we conclude, is simply a part of human nature. While denial can be deliberate and quite conscious—an outright lie—Steven Cohen in his *States of Denial* reports a psychological theory of denial "as an unconscious defense mechanism for coping with guilt, anxiety and other disturbing emotions aroused by reality. The psyche blocks off information that is literally unthinkable or unbearable. The unconscious sets up a barrier which prevents the thought from reaching conscious knowledge."[1]

Jean-Paul Sartre, on the other hand, speaks of denial as "bad faith," a conscious slight of hand that keeps "secret" a reality we are unwilling to acknowledge.[2] A classic example of bad faith occurred during the 1990s as the U.S. bishops cautiously faced the scandal of clergy abuse of minors. A group of scholars proposed to the bishops that a study be undertaken to determine the psychological, social, and developmental causes of the behavior that was so tragically betraying and wounding countless young Catholics. The proposed study was blocked, according to reports, by a few American cardinals who believed such a study would call too much attention to the problem of clergy abuse. A decade later the bad faith of these church authorities has contributed to a scandal shaking the very foundations of the church. Fear of "too much attention" has led, as we shall see in chapter six, to an avalanche of attention—to a scandal of unprecedented proportions. When bad faith is found in church leaders who preach commitment to the truth, such leaders betray the gospel they proclaim and the people—and children—they are called to serve.

The very nature of bad faith makes it invisible, and we choose to make it invisible. Like children closing their eyes to a disturbing scene, we turn away. We instinctively, mindlessly, turn away. We pretend not to see, not to hear. It might, as we have seen, call *too much attention to a problem, it might harm the reputation of the church, of the priesthood.* And then we would have to be responsible. We don't see the elephant in the room because we aren't ready to accept the tension, even pain, which inevitably follows upon seeing it. Furthermore, we are afraid to take the appropriate action that the elephant's presence demands.

The denial of painful realities, whether personal or institutional, and the decision to go about one's business as if the problem or situation did not exist, leads to existential guilt. The human soul remains restless and ill at ease. Not conscious of deliberate wrongdoing, the soul feels guilty without knowing why. It is not unreasonable to see a link here with addictive behaviors. Food, drink, drugs, power, control—all effect a blurring of awareness that quiets the unease of existential guilt.

Much of the denial evident in the church today, I believe, is rightly understood as a form of "bad faith," though the psychological theory proposing an unconscious dynamic is also likely to be operative. Both forms may be triggered, as we noted in the previous chapter, by a misguided sense of loyalty or responsibility and fueled by a suspicion of the unpleasant consequences that would likely follow if the denial were not sustained. Understood from the perspective of "bad faith," denial and minimization are signs of moral cowardice, of failed courage. It works something like this: we sense something is wrong, but we know well the mind of our superiors, and, rather than risk the loss of standing in the good graces of those in authority—sometimes without any explicit decision to do so—we maintain silence. The anxiety and fear fueling the various forms of denial, rather than being linked to an individual's place in the institution, can be traced, in some cases, to the need to protect the image or authority of the institution. More often than not, ecclesial manifestations of denial evoke little conscious guilt. They do, however, chip away at the integrity of individuals and institutions when such behaviors are employed. Nor do I see Machiavellian motives lurking behind the denials and half-truths evident in the church today although they cannot be ruled out completely.

Especially prone to the dynamics of denial are individuals whose identity and self-worth are determined by the expectations of others, especially others who have positions of authority over them. For these individuals, being perceived as a loyal soldier in one's thinking and external behavior is of vital importance. Personal experiences and convictions not in harmony with the controlling institutional culture evoke considerable anxiety and are carefully guarded lest they be discovered. Inevitably, the individual so on guard succumbs to the mechanisms of denial.[3] In so doing the one who denies—or the institution that denies—commences an unholy game of selected blindness. Others are drawn into the game, reinforcing the timid and cowing individuals who sense in their bones that the game is rigged. Those who refuse to play are labeled disloyal, troublemakers, mavericks. Often they are shunned by others who have staked their present status—and their futures—on playing the game with calculating skill. The game is never-ending, the players come and go, the elephant remains invisible, and moral courage evaporates.

Accountability

Especially in hierarchical institutions like the church, accountability is, for the most part, upward: the priest is accountable to his bishop, his bishop is accountable to the pope, and the pope is accountable to God. The idea of accountability to one's hierarchical inferiors is simply dismissed out of hand. It would imply that the hierarchical order itself might be of human institution rather than divine. Moreover, such accountability, it is feared, would weaken the authority of those in leadership roles. From a theological and biblical perspective, of course, fidelity to the Word of God and the mutual accountability manifested in the church understood as communion reveal the limitations of any purely upward model. Still, from a psychological perspective, hierarchical models of accountability by their very nature foster mechanisms of denial. Inferiors on the hierarchical ladder strive to exemplify the institution's values and teachings and repress or deny any anxiety-provoking realities that appear to be in conflict with these values or teachings. Superiors, on the other hand, may feel little obligation to seek advice or to explain the factors that have shaped their decisions, even decisions affecting the lives of others, and tend to deny their mistakes in judgment or personal failures. Acknowledging mistakes and wrongdoing and holding themselves accountable, it is feared, might undermine their ability to govern. It is, therefore, rather surprising to hear a pastor apologize to parishioners, a bishop apologize to priests, a pope apologize to bishops.

In a remarkable turn of protocol, apologies for the mistakes and failings of the church in ages past have distinguished the papacy of John Paul II. The church's consistent tendency, however, to various forms of deceit and denial is demonstrated in Gary Wills' compelling book, *Papal Sin: Structures of Deceit*.[4] Institutions, even institutions claiming to be guardians of revealed truths and to enjoy the special guidance of God's spirit, display an *institutional instinct* that makes their first priority the enhancement of the organization and the reinforcement of the organization's authority. Thus an unholy dissimulation runs through much of its public discourse when the church is confronted with various forms of scandal perpetrated by its own personnel. It behaves instinctively the way institutions behave. And it behaves with the belief that its dissimulations and "spins" are "for the good of the church." Examples of such strategies follow in chapter six, "Abuse of our Children" and chapter seven, "Clerical Culture."

When institutional denial is no longer tenable because of the dissemination of conflicting realities or facts, church spokespersons often turn to minimization and contextualization. The latter strategy is often appropriate and necessary but just as often projects the church in a defensive posture. Lateral or horizontal structures of accountability and mutual responsibility, on the other hand, although still prone to the dynamics of denial, diminish its occurrence.

Presumptive Denial

Church traditions that have stayed the course of time are particularly difficult to review, let alone challenge. If certain disciplines or practices have been in place for years, even centuries, it is presumed that they merit uncritical continuation. During my years of study for the priesthood, I remember a fellow seminarian respectfully asking a professor if the clerical practice of accepting money from parishioners for the offering of Mass for their intentions didn't smack of simony. The curt response surprised me. In a tone that betrayed considerable anger, the professor rebuffed the seminarian for presuming to challenge a long-standing, honorable church tradition, which, the professor implied, was to be honored because it was a long-standing practice in the church. The question, by the way, deserves to be asked again. And it deserves a thoughtful, respectful answer.

There is, of course, something to be said for longevity. If something has worked and worked for generations, even centuries, possible changes to the practice or procedure should be carefully thought through lest the good or value inherent in such practices and procedures be lost. But to deny the need for periodic review of church practices and disciplines—Mass stipends and mandatory celibacy, for example—is a failure to trust the workings of the Spirit in each and every age of the church.

Historical Denial

I remember being surprised to learn that a number of bishops during America's colonial period owned slaves. I was equally surprised when I was informed that young women entering the convent from land-owning families during the same period often brought with them personal slaves.[5] These sobering realities never quite made it into the American history courses that marked my secondary and college education. Nor did the church's major blunders receive the attention they deserved during my seminary studies. We students of Catholic schools heard abridged and sanitized versions of the Crusades, the Inquisition, the church's use of torture, papal greed and decadence, cultural dissimulations by missionaries, and the church's anti-Semitism. We heard about Protestant bigotry against Catholics, but little of Catholic bigotry directed towards later immigrant groups and those who did not share our faith. We heard about the moral superiority of Americans, about our generous rebuilding of Europe at the conclusion of

World War II, but little about the exploitation of native Americans, the detention of Japanese Americans, the carpet bombing of German cities, or the decision to use not one, but two, atomic bombs. Whether telling our ecclesial, national, or our personal stories, we speak, of course, from our own perspective, and with a keen awareness of our own righteousness and God's special blessing. It can be no other way as the histories of nations and peoples make clear. What can be different, however, is a willingness to concede our inherent tendency to denial and minimization. Souls, the souls of individuals and societies, expand when they respect and acknowledge this tendency.

Personal Denial

If there is an institutional instinct toward denial, there most certainly is a personal one. Especially during retreats and moments given to honest self-evaluation, we are likely to see the significant role denial plays in our lives. It not only lurks in the corners of our moral and ethical choices, our failures to be women and men of charity, hope, and faith, but it can be seen shading our individual, semiconscious appraisals. "Maybe I do eat or drink a *little* too much." "Maybe I do work a *little* too hard—or not hard enough." "Maybe I am a *little* self-centered and thoughtless." It seems so very human to soften, minimize, and deny. From time to time the human spirit needs the comfort that follows upon rounding the edges of reality. In many cases it seems harmless enough. On the other hand, addiction counselors remind us of the devastating harm that unchecked denial and minimization can wreak. St. Augustine understood deliverance from such denial when he wrote, "Lord, you turned my attention back to myself. You took me up from behind my own back where I had placed myself because I did not wish to observe myself, and you set me before my face."[6] And so we pray (fervently, lamely?) to know ourselves as we are, as we stand in the light of truth, as God's beloved sons and daughters. We are as sick as our secrets, twelve-step veterans remind us. An exaggeration, perhaps, but still an insight that merits thoughtful consideration. Even victims of abuse, both domestic and institutional, regularly deny or minimize the violence they suffer. Feeling helpless and powerless, a strategy of denial is thought to be the only means of survival. Compounding their suffering, victims adapt enabling and codependent behaviors in their attempts to cope with their abuse.[7] They count their blessings, take comfort when they hear of victims whose abuse appears far worse than their own, reflect on the good qualities of the abuser and the benefits the abusing individual or institution provides. Feeling afraid and trapped, they convince themselves that their situations aren't so bad. Not surprisingly, breaking through such denial often demands heroic moral courage.

Perpetrators of abuse, again not surprisingly, are often masters of denial. What is done, although "perhaps morally ambiguous," is thought to somehow benefit the victim. Consider the example of an admitted abuser, Cleveland priest Neil Conway:

> Conway convinced himself he was involved in an intense friendship. So extreme was his denial that he claims it never occurred to him that his actions were inappropriate, much less illegal. He only remembers feeling the most profound sort of love. That is common, says [psychotherapist and author A. Richard] Sipe, who has treated perpetrators in the clergy. "The real resistance to treatment for people with this condition is their belief they're not hurting the kids. . . . They tell themselves, 'I love them' or 'I'm helping them because they don't have a father or they're poor.'"[8]

Witnesses and observers of abuse and other forms of injustice also employ strategies of denial. Fear of becoming involved, fear of the consequences that are likely to follow decisive action to halt the specific injustice, foster a "see no evil, hear no evil, speak no evil" attitude. The responsibility to stop the harm being done, so the reasoning goes, is somebody else's. Or, especially in cases of systemic patterns or policies infringing on the rights of others, it is determined that speaking out against a given wrong would be futile: "My voice wouldn't make a difference."

Our various personal denials, sometimes innocent, sometimes sick, and sometimes evil, allow us to consider the institutional church's denials with a certain compassion and forbearance. Which is indeed appropriate. At the same time, the moral courage required to face our individual catalogue of denials is similar to the moral courage required of the church's leaders to work through the institution's denials and unholy silences. It is precisely here that we come to see there is no authentic faith without real courage and that there is always something heroic in the heart of every sincere believer. Only a passion for the truth, both personal and collective, only an openness to the Spirit of truth, offers the promise of freedom, health, and ultimate salvation.

PART TWO

FACES OF DENIAL

CHAPTER THREE

SACRED OATHS, SACRED PROMISES

You have heard that it was said to those of ancient times, "You shall not swear falsely, but carry out the vows you have made to the Lord." But I say to you, Do not swear at all, either by heaven, for it is the throne of God, or by the earth, for it is his footstool, or be Jerusalem, for it is the city of the great King. And do not swear by your head, for you cannot make one hair white or black. Let your word be "Yes, Yes" or "No, No"; anything more than this comes from the evil one.

—Matthew 5:33-37

The sword is not so piercing as the nature of an oath!
The sabre is not so destructive as the stroke of an oath!
The swearer, although he seems to live is already dead,
and has received the fatal blow.

—John Chrysostom

AS I BEGAN THE FINAL YEAR OF STUDIES leading to my ordination as priest, my classmates and I were informed that church law required clerics (tonsured seminarians) to take the oath against Modernism prior to ordination. The oath, in effect since 1910, was to be taken not only by seminarians approaching ordination but also by all those being appointed confessors, preachers, pastors, seminary professors, religious superiors, and major diocesan and Vatican officials. It was instituted by Pope Pius X to assure the demise of "Modernism, the synthesis of all heresies," which he had condemned in his 1907 encyclical *Pascendi dominici gregis*.[1] With this oath, a cleric vowed submission to the teachings of the 1907 decree of the Holy Office *Lamentabili*, "which condemned sixty-five Modernist propositions on the nature of the church, on revelation, on the person of Christ, and on the sacraments, and to the encyclical *Pascendi dominici gregis*, which elaborated on these themes."[2] Commenting on *Pascendi dominici*, John Tracy Ellis noted that:

> [T]he paranoia the encyclical ignited spread rapidly. Seminary curriculum was often reduced to a series of questions and answers, questions that had not been asked in centuries. Students were expected to simply memorize everything. "Catholic philosophy alone has the truth," one professor wrote. He echoed what others thought or practiced. Students developed the weakest of all attitudes toward adversaries—one of contempt.[3]

Not only contempt, I might add, but seminarians assumed there was nothing to learn from the "adversaries" who were seldom treated by seminary professors prior to Vatican II with any kind of respect. Mistaken they may have been, but judged today in light of contemporary theological and scriptural scholarship, they pointed to insights and truths that a less defensive mindset should have been able to acknowledge even then. The adversaries, mostly European Protestant scholars, were simply dismissed as enemies of the faith. In addition to contempt, I believe Ellis would agree, seminarians were steeped in an attitude and atmosphere of triumphalism. This attitude, according to Ellis, "lasted well into our day."

> The conceit of the clergy was terrible. Some priests, ordained between 1915 and 1929, and interviewed in 1969, stated that they felt they had received a superior education, despite the fact that their education required little reading and less research. The seminary library was opened only two hours a day.[4]

Not only did the oath against Modernism tragically weaken the academic training of priests, it deepened an already profound

suspicion of human experience. Only the official sources mattered—only the voice of authority. According to Kilian McDonnell:

> The condemnations of modernism at the turn of the century cre-
> ated a magisterial distrust of the appeal to experience in theology,
> experience being seen narrowly in psychological or subjectivist
> terms. This pushed a wedge between Catholic theology and those
> contemporary historical, social, scientific, and cultural expressions
> of experience. This meant that theology floated in an ahistorical
> stratosphere, handing on Scripture, tradition, and the scholastic
> synthesis, with the argument from authority being the absolute,
> isolated from its social context.[5]

It was in this kind of atmosphere that I began my seminary
study of theology. These years, from 1961 to 1965, coincided with
the four sessions of Vatican II. While my theology training was influenced to some extent by the conciliar documents that appeared
during these years of study, my education and formation were de-
cidedly pre-conciliar. At the same time, my classmates and I were
well aware of the major themes and new directions embraced by
the council. We followed carefully and with considerable excitement the media reports and commentaries of bishops, theologians,
and journalists that signaled the epochal theological transitions at
the heart of the council. Many of these themes and new directions,
I discovered, stood in stark contrast to the theological positions and
declarations found in the antimodernist oath. I mention here but
one example. In contrast to the well-established understanding of
the evolution or development of doctrine, the oath against Modernism called for the person taking the oath to swear: *"I sincerely
receive the teaching of faith as transmitted in the same sense and
meaning right down to us; and, therefore, I wholly reject the
heretical notion of the evolution of dogmas, which pass from one
sense to another alien to that the Church held from the start; and
I likewise condemn every error whereby is substituted for divine
deposit, entrusted by Christ to His spouse and by her to be faithfully guarded, a philosophic system or a creation of the human*

conscience, gradually refined by the striving of men and finally to be perfected hereafter by indefinite progress."[6]

With ordination only months away, I wrestled with a serious conflict of conscience. I was being asked to swear to uphold theological and doctrinal positions that were being transcended if not repudiated by the council fathers. Furthermore, those called to ministry as priests, we seminarians understood, were entrusted with the word of God. Tending this word through preaching, study, and teaching was central, even primary, to our ministry as presbyters.[7] As disciples of Christ and his gospel, our personal word was at the heart of our integrity as "bearers of the word." There was to be something sacred about the word of a priest. Oaths, we knew from our childhood, were sacred by their very nature. And so, my conscience was disturbed. My credibility and integrity as a priest, I knew full well, would be grounded in the truth of the words I spoke, especially words sworn to under oath.

In the swirl of these emotions almost forty years ago, I remember only an unsettling silence from my seminary professors. They had to understand that placing the oath in front of us to sign would trigger a crisis in conscience. Yet there was no acknowledgment of the turmoil that I suspect many of us felt. No counsel about how we might resolve our dilemma, how we might ease our troubled consciences. Did they understand our moral crisis? And if they did, did they simply not care? I suspect now that the faculty themselves were in a state of denial. The church required the oath against Modernism for those about to be ordained. In spite of the dramatic new directions taken by the council fathers, the requirement had not been rescinded. They believed, it seems to me, that they had little discretion in the matter. As seminary professors they were men of obedience with the responsibility of teaching their charges to be men of obedience.[8] And so they were silent and in their silence entered into a sacred conspiracy of denial.

I took the oath. My classmates took the oath. I remember little if any discussion about it among ourselves. We entered, it seems now, into our own conspiracy of denial. The oath was put before us. We were expected to sign it. We did sign it. What a conflicted, ambiguous beginning to our ministry of proclaiming God's saving, liberating word to the world. Certainly, there was some coercion present—the very proximity to sacred orders exerted its own pressure. But we were men in our mid-twenties, old enough to think for ourselves, to stand our ground. Our acquiescence, it seems to me, was brought about by some of the same factors that lie just below the surface of our current culture of denial. We seminarians wanted to think of ourselves as loyal and responsible individuals. We wanted our last months of seminary life to be marked with at least relative tranquility. This was not the time to "make waves." Add to that a fear of the consequences—disappointment by some, criticism by others, the risk of jeopardizing a goal we had been preparing to attain for many years—and you have the core ingredients to a collective act of denial.

The oath, by the way, wasn't rescinded until July 1967.[9] I wonder how the ordination classes of 1966 and 1967 handled the dilemma of the oath. Perhaps the more fundamental question has to do with the council fathers themselves. As they processed into St. Peter's Basilica for the opening session of Vatican II, did any of them recall the import of the oath they themselves had taken against Modernism? Did it affect their deliberations, their interventions? Did they ever pause while reading the various drafts of the constitutions, decrees, and declarations of the council and acknowledge that what they held in their hands transgressed, in many cases, the tenents of the oath they had taken many years before? No doubt many of the reactionary bishops did, but I suspect most of the council fathers understood the Spirit was present and calling for a fresh look at the church in the modern world. And they acted accordingly.

The Profession of Faith and the Oath of Fidelity

Before ordination, today's seminarians are required to make both a profession of faith and an oath of fidelity.[10] Similar ecclesial oaths and professions can be traced to the very origins of the church. Our "Christian tradition has always considered a profession of faith sacrosanct: a declaration of surrender to the truth divinely revealed."[11] The profession of faith, of course, is an essential component of the rite of baptism. It is the public form of our covenant with God in Jesus Christ and the power of the Spirit. We confirm our public profession of faith at every celebration of the Eucharist, especially the Sunday celebration, and at least implicitly, at every gathering of the church for prayer and praise, at every moment when we strive to meet the needs of our brothers and sisters in the name of the gospel.

In light of these multiple affirmations of faith, what, we might ask, is really going on when the church requires baptized and confirmed adults to again swear their allegiance not only to Jesus Christ and the church, but also to adhere with religious submission of will and intellect to church teachings proclaimed "in an act that is not definitive"?[12] Clearly, concern for the preservation of the authentic tradition of the church motivates the legislation of these professions and oaths. At least in part, I am convinced, they also are intended to assure an external, if not internal, conformity in matters of church teaching, even teachings that are not "definitively" put forth by the teaching office of the church. Sincere and committed Christians sense their own thinking about and reflecting on the truths and teachings of the faith is being curtailed. What is being called for, they believe, is their silent acquiescence to what is proposed simply because it is proposed by church authorities. Ladislas Örsy, no doubt, spoke for a multitude of thinking Catholics when he asked:

> [T]his is our question, how can the human mind affirm that a proposition is true when its truth is neither witnessed by the Holy Spirit nor supported by rational evidence? The intellect, to be what it is, and to be faithful to its own nature, must somehow "see" the truth. This happens when the Spirit enhances its capacity to perceive the presence of a mystery. This happens when a judgment is made on the strength of compelling evidence. In either case the in-

tellect surrenders to the truth. But how can that happen when neither the light of faith nor the light of reason is postulated?[13]

Oaths of fidelity, like the loyalty oaths characteristic of the early and middle decades of the twentieth-century in the U.S., initially may lead to periods of fearful silence and external conformity, but seldom change the minds and hearts of the individuals called upon to take them.[14] Our history as a church reveals the profoundly ambiguous nature of the oath. Condemned by Jesus of Nazareth in Matthew 5, in the Epistle of James, chapter 5, by Augustine and Chrysostom, the use of oaths was, nonetheless, confirmed by Thomas Aquinas as "not only licit but good, though he warned that oaths could be misused and therefore should be sworn only out of necessity and with due caution."[15] Thomas' warning deserves careful heeding: Oaths "should be sworn only out of necessity and with due caution." A seminarian's troubled conscience pales in light of the considerable harm and suffering occasioned by the oath against Modernism for numerous theologians and clerics at the turn of the twentieth century. Rectors were removed, faculties disbanded, the highly respected theological journal, *The New York Review*, was suppressed.[16] Aware of the abuses that still impact negatively the intellectual lives of numerous priests and bishops, the regular use of oaths and professions of faith warrants careful review:

> [B]oth professions of faith and oaths are easily subject to misuse, not only through apostasy and perjury, or through coercion and fear, but also in more prosaic ways; for example, the perfunctory recitation of creeds can easily foster indifferentism, while the casual swearing of oaths or their coercion effectively trivializes them.[17]

In light of the council's avowed respect for modernity and with all of the implications that follow upon the council's new directions, it can be said today that the oath against Modernism simply didn't work. In the meantime, as we have seen, it ruined the personal and professional lives of countless theologians, seminary

professors, pastors, and thinking Catholics in general. It smoth-
ered the intellectual vitality of the church on both sides of the Atlantic, which in turn had significant, even devastating, pastoral
consequences because of the truncated and skewed seminary education to which generations of priests were subjected. In the
minds of more than a few American educators, we were informed,
the term "Catholic university" was thought to be an oxymoron.

Finally, I need to ask: Is it possible in the present climate of
fear, control, and denial that we may see the day when church authorities call for seminarians and other church officials to take an
oath against postmodernism? Do we have the seeds of such an
oath in the *mandatum* for Catholic theology professors called for
by John Paul II's apostolic letter *Ex corde ecclesiae?* These questions are, by no means, endorsements of the various manifestations of what has been loosely labeled "postmodernism," which
we will discuss in chapter four in terms of its impact on religious
vocations. I believe the church has yet to comprehend the challenges and opportunities that this emerging, amorphous episte-
mological view holds in store for religious belief in general and
Catholicism in particular. The wrong place to begin, I propose, is
with yet another oath.

Sacred Promises

Oaths and professions of faith are promises writ large. When
we make them, their sacred character defines our personal integrity and shapes our personal identity. They make us who we
are. But so do other promises: the promises of fidelity made by a
man and woman celebrating the commitment of marriage; the
solemn vows of religious consecration; the promise of the newly
ordained priest to respect and obey his bishop. These public commitments as well as the personal promises known only to a few
likewise shape the character of our souls. How we honor them or
betray them becomes the story line of our lives. We turn to them
now because they illumine the workings of grace in the lives of

those who are faithful to their words of promise—often to the point of heroic courage—and because they shed light on the tenacity and resilience common to the various manifestations of denial evident in the church.

Earlier we examined the dialectical nature of the church's mission to the world, in particular, the creative tension held in place by the authoritative teachings of the church and the lived experiences of women and men of faith. It is the faithful's experience of fidelity and betrayal, of grace and estrangement, and of communion and alienation that provides the context out of which they respond to and receive the official teachings of the church. Without the "reception" of a church teaching by the people of God, the teaching remains unconfirmed.[18] As Christians reflect on their fidelity to the promises they have made, especially those promises made *as* Christians, their understanding of God's fidelity to them—their understanding of the covenant relationship inaugurated by the creator—is deepened and purified. It is this experience of God's saving fidelity that qualifies them to speak to the church of their own truth and to receive or not receive official church teachings.

Thus, human experience deserves to be valued, even cherished, by church authorities. The people of God as well as the teaching office of the church are submerged in a sea of grace. Both voices deserve to be heard with reverence and openness. The weight I am placing here on the experience of grace prompted by the promises and commitments we make is greeted in many quarters of the church with considerable suspicion. Margaret Farley rightly observes:

To think that such a focus [on the experience of commitment] turns us in upon ourselves, preoccupied with our own "experience," unable or refusing to open to God's own self or even to one another as sharers in the human community, is to miss the inner potential of our experience. Neither God nor other human persons are reducible to our experience of them; but in our experience may lie the promise of transcendence of ourselves, of access to communion and friendship.[19]

Our fidelity to the promises we make reveals the contours of our souls and the mystery of grace which sustains us in discipleship. But all of our promises must be consistent with the fundamental promise of fidelity to God in Jesus Christ and the power of the Spirit. And here is the rub. Bernard Haring, a theologian distinguished for his obedience and fidelity, speaks of the crisis that occurs when fidelity to conscience conflicts with promises made to obey church authorities:

> Religious obedience has quite an exceptional dignity. In its absolute form, we owe religious obedience to God alone. But just as God's revelation comes to us only when mediated, so too, the truths of faith reach us only when mediated. The meaning of faith and the authenticity of religious obedience confront a crisis when religious authorities . . . demand all too much submission to an obscure package of doctrines.[20]

The tensions inherent in authentic religious obedience, as Haring implies, can lead to painful crises of conscience. Many parish priests suffered such a crisis with the publication in 1968 of Paul VI's encyclical *Humanae vitae*. Most priests remained silent, at least publicly. But not all. In the Archdiocese of Washington, alone, dozens of priests, in spite of their promise to obey their bishop, refused to sign a statement promising to embrace and uphold the teachings against artificial birth control proclaimed in Paul VI's encyclical. Their decision to remain faithful to what they considered a more fundamental promise led to their suspension as active priests. The majority of their diocesan brothers, however, chose to be obedient to their bishop who, no doubt, believed he was simply holding fast to his promise to be obedient to the bishop of Rome. Many did so in good conscience; I suspect many others did so with a very troubled conscience.

The situation just outlined reveals the shadow side of the promise of obedience. If an individual's promise to obey is not mature, he or she is likely to turn away from the hard work of facing the kind of crisis described above by Haring. Relief is often found by reducing the complexity of the crisis to a matter of simple obedience to one's proximate ecclesial superior. When this is the case, integrity suffers.

A short time ago a priest I know went to visit one of his former seminary professors, now up in years and seriously ill. My friend sensed his former teacher was quite disturbed. His intuition was borne out when the older man asked his former student, now a theologian, if he could turn the conversation to a matter that was acutely painful to him. He had plenty of time to think, he said, in his twilight years and his thoughts kept returning to his post-seminary assignment as a pastor. Both as a counselor and confessor, he had been firm and insistent upon official church teaching when husbands and wives had approached him for guidance about the birth control issue. He saw the matter differently now. He felt he had been too legalistic, too unbending, as a pastor and, to his credit, he neither minimized nor denied the anguish his strict obedience to the church's teaching had no doubt caused his parishioners.

Now, before the eyes of his young friend, he gave words to the inner conversion that was silently renewing his pastoral integrity and his peace of soul. While not a conversion from sin to virtue in the strict sense of what we understand as formal sin, it was indeed a conversion of heart and mind, a turn from a "letter of the law" legalism to a more compassionate, pastoral understanding of the confusion and guilt that was troubling many of his parishioners. In such conversions, which I believe are numerous, priests deepen their commitment to the gospel and honor the promise they made to shepherd and nourish the people of God.

It seems likely that the elderly pastor was grieving his earlier denial of his own pastoral experience and the experience of his people. Few things, I'm convinced, renew and expand our souls as much as honest grieving. For whenever we honestly grieve our mistakes and failures, our limits and losses, there can be no denying, no blinking to the truth we know in our hearts. My friend acknowledged how moved he was as he left his former professor's room. Honest human feeling does that. The grief he was privileged to witness was real and necessary if his friend was to live out his life in peace of soul. Perhaps the elderly priest was never more a professor than when he bared his soul to a former student who simply stopped by to say hello and to see how he was doing.

Our promises and how we hold to them, it seems clear, lead us to integrity of soul or to the dis-ease of denial, to the light of that which is real or to the shadow reality of rationalization. The women and men who have been initiated into the communion of the church through baptism, confirmation, and Eucharist, have solemnly promised to carry the light of Christ to the world in the power of the Holy Spirit. They have sworn an oath—made a profession of faith. Our understanding of this marvelous, implausible mission will continue to develop in the years and centuries ahead. So it has been promised. We make a serious mistake when, by sacred oath or sacred promise, we try to make our present understanding of the church and its teachings incapable of further insight and development—when we try to freeze them in time. That is precisely what we do when we require additional sacred oaths and sacred promises. In this light multiple sacred oaths and sacred promises occasioned by threatening circumstances seem to be misguided attempts to make static (and secure) that which is alive and unfolding by the grace and power of the Holy Spirit.

CHAPTER FOUR

VOICES OF WOMEN

Speak the truth in love.

—Catherine of Siena

Women in contemporary churches are suffering from linguistic depri-
vation and eucharistic famine. They can no longer nurture their souls in
alienating words that ignore or systematically deny their existence. . . .

—Rosemary Ruether, *Women–Church*

I AM AWARE OF THE PITFALLS I FACE reflecting on the church's pro-
clivity to exclude the voices of women from the discourse that
shapes its self-understanding, its pastoral care, and its prophetic
mission. I cannot speak from their experience. I cannot transcend
my gender, my experience as a presbyter, nor the historicity of my
time and culture. Still, in spite of the significant limitations just
mentioned, the issue deserves to be addressed because, among
other reasons, an ecclesial culture that mutes the voices of women
is significantly impoverished since God's voice may be heard in
their experience, expertise, and wisdom. Perhaps one more voice
might bring us closer to the "tipping point" I believe we are approaching relentlessly if ever so slowly.

Increasing numbers of women and men are coming to see that
the perennial muting of women's voices inhibits the church from
serving as fully as it might as a beacon of light and hope to its own
members and beyond. Especially since the renewal of Vatican II, it
is acknowledged with a certain sense of enlightened awareness that
the whole people of God—men *and* women—have been anointed

by the Spirit. When the church listens and when the church speaks, therefore, it should be with the ears and tongues of both men and women. Of course, we would be equally impoverished as a church if the voices of men were restricted in the same manner that women's voices are. But one can hardly imagine that.

It can be argued, certainly, that never before have the voices of women been heard with such regularity and clarity as in this turn-of-the-millennium period of history. With heretofore unimaginable opportunities for graduate and professional education and having mastered the communication technologies of the last decades of the twentieth century, they speak and write more effectively and freely than ever before. While they hold positions of leadership in government, education, commerce, and most of the professions that make them effective participants in the discourse and decisions that shape our culture, they hold, for the most part, relatively few leadership positions in the church.

There is clear evidence, reports Dolores Leckey, former executive director of the Secretariat for Family, Laity, Women and Youth, at the National Conference of Catholic Bishops, that women are indeed assuming roles of significant leadership in the church. While they represent but a small portion of the church's leadership pie, the evolving trend has led some of these women to profess "hopeful realism" about future roles of leadership for women:

> In March 2001 an unusual consultation was held in Chicago. Sponsored by the Bishops' Committee on Women in Society and in the Church, about 150 women—church executives in a variety of roles—gathered to review the recent research on women like themselves: chancellors and school superintendents, social ministry directors, chief financial officers, and a host of other positions. The women (vowed religious and lay) revealed a new profile of diocesan leadership across the country. They came with the backing of their bishops and spoke with the authority that comes from competence, experience, and wisdom. Their voices were those of hopeful realism.[1]

A Prayer of AIM for Monastic Life

O loving God,
we ask your blessing
on all monastic men and women,
especially those who live and work
in the most destitute parts of the world.

Help them to become people of prayer and peace.
May they be visible signs
that strangers can live together in God's love.
Give them hearts wide enough
to welcome the traveler, the outcast,
the neighbor.
Enable them to listen to and learn from
the people they serve,
especially the poorest.
May their communities be models
of wise stewardship, of dignified human labor,
of sacred leisure, and
of reverence for all living things.

Above all, O God,
may a monastic presence in the world
be a constant witness of justice,
compassion and hope to all.
Amen.

Mary Lou Kownacki, OSB

Copies of this prayer card are available from:
AIM USA • 345 East Ninth Street • Erie, PA 16503-1107 • USA
(814)453-4724 • www.aim-usa.org • aim@aim-usa.org

Leckey also notes that the vast majority of parish ministers are women. "Not only are Catholic women laboring alongside diocesan bishops, they account for 83 percent of U.S. Catholic parish ministers."[2] In spite of gains in some executive corridors, women continue to search for venues that would allow them to address the issues and concerns of church life that affect them and their families as well as those issues and concerns affecting the church as a whole.

To a lesser extent, of course, this is true for men in the church who are not ordained. It is also true in the lower ranks of Catholic clergy. In the latter case, frustration and even anger surface when priests discuss their public meetings with church authorities (e.g., clergy convocations and meetings of priests' councils) which are structured in ways that tend to inhibit open and free dialogue. My focus here, however, is on the systems and structures of the church that play a significant role in turning a deaf ear to women's voices, especially the voices of women religious and women theologians.

This reflection on the church's denial, at least in practice, of the significance and importance of women's voices is grounded in my pastoral and personal encounters for more than three decades now with significant numbers of women who remain clearly committed to the church. Their fidelity to the gospel and to the covenants forged in marriage vows and religious profession was beyond question. I also came to know single women whose lives of service and quiet loyalty often went unnoticed. Many were colleagues in ministry or education, others served with me in diocesan leadership roles, and still others proved to be spiritual guides and life-long friends. What follows here, to a great extent, has been shaped by the grace of their lives and by conversations that have been ongoing, in a few cases, for almost half a century. Some will certainly hear echoes of their insights and sentiments in the pages that follow. While acknowledging my debt to these women of the church, I speak for myself and welcome their insights and correctives as part of the process that challenges and critiques male hegemony.

Reflecting on these conversations with committed Catholic women and on the writings of women theologians, I became aware of the limits of my own understanding and my need to re-think the vision of church that was part and parcel of my seminary training. Conversations with women theologians and others dented my own denial and blindness to the structural inequities and injustices that could be found at the heart of the church, both universal and local. I write here, then, as one whose conversion of mind and heart is in process.

In conversation after conversation with committed Catholic women about issues and challenges facing the church in general and the role of women in particular, I could not miss the under-currents of frustration, hurt, and anger. But more arresting than their anger and hurt, was their profound sadness—a sadness ema-nating from the realization that, in practice, church and papal documents notwithstanding, male voices alone continued to shape the decisions and policies, the very culture and personality of the church.[3] I heard of urgent desires to hear the word of God preached by voices similar to their own. They could find no compelling ra-tionale for the law of the church permitting male voices alone to preach at Mass thereby limiting the Word of God to an exclusively male perspective.

Women religious express their sadness—and understandable anger—at not being able to choose one of their own, a sister edu-cated and trained to proclaim God's word, to preach at the jubilee and funeral liturgies of their sisters. Even vowed religious, trained at the doctoral level in preaching and in some cases teaching homiletics to seminarians, are prohibited from preaching the ju-bilee or funeral homilies for sisters in their congregation.[4] Often their anger goes unexpressed; their sadness and discouragement, however, are quite palpable.

Chancery staffs, as we have seen, and the staffs of some Vati-can congregations do indeed include women. Their numbers are such, however, that they represent only a small percentage of the people sitting at the table. While the church authorities insist that women should be included at all levels of the institutional church not prohibited by canon law, women continue to be woefully underrepresented.

The Failed Pastoral

In the early 1980s, recognizing the mounting tension surrounding the role of women in the church, the National Conference of Catholic Bishops decided to move forward with a proposal to write a pastoral letter on women's concerns. Bishop Joseph Imesch, then chair of the NCCB's Committee on Women, was asked to chair the pastoral letter committee as well—arguably the most challenging and exhausting assignment ever accepted by a U.S. bishop. In the months that followed women expressed their hopes and concerns, their frustrations and discouragement at listening sessions held by a number of diocesan bishops in preparation for the planned pastoral.[5] The hope and expectations inspired by these sessions was eventually dampened when successive drafts of the pastoral were found unacceptable by the bishops and large numbers of women themselves.

When the first of four drafts appeared, titled, "Partners in the Mystery of Redemption," "[I]t didn't look like other pastorals," Dolores Leckey observed. "It started with the voices of women, followed by church teaching, and then the bishops' response to the interaction between experience and tradition."[6] But immediately there was trouble. "There were rumblings about the name, the process, and the format. Opponents claimed that a new sin had been introduced, the sin of sexism. . . . By the time the final draft was presented to the bishops' meeting in November 1992, it was clear that while a majority would vote for the pastoral, the two-thirds vote necessary for passage simply fell short."[7] It was the only pastoral letter the NCCB ever defeated.

The drafting of the letter had taken its toll on the writing committee, especially on its courageous chair, Bishop Imesch. Presenting the fourth and final draft to the bishops before their historic vote, Imesch said, "How history will judge our efforts during these past nine years may be disputed. What cannot be disputed is the fact that women have very deeply felt and legitimate concerns—concerns that range from abuse at home, less than equal standing in society, and in many ways, less than equal standing in the Church."[8]

A telling insight related to the pastoral letter came from Bishop P. Francis Murphy who noted that "the most serious concern raised by Vatican officials [regarding the proposed U.S. Bishops' Pastoral on Women's Concerns] was the consultation process. . . . They asserted that bishops are teachers, not learners; truth cannot emerge through consultation."[9] Especially in light of the conciliar documents, it is clear that bishops can indeed be learners—they *must* be learners and not only from each other. Pope Paul VI in his apostolic exhortation *Evangelization in the Modern World*, reminded the church that evangelizers themselves first need to be evangelized and this again and again. Certainly included here would be deacons, priests, and bishops. This means that church authorities and preachers are called upon to develop listening hearts, hearts open to insight and wisdom that might surface even from the most humble and simple of God's people. Such holy listening prepares the soul for transformation and conversion. But priests and bishops have been conditioned to engage in a different kind of listening, a listening that certainly has its place yet remains woefully inadequate for effective leadership and preaching. This is the kind of listening that is alert to the nature and implications of a question so that one might offer an informed and wise answer. Closely allied to this form of clerical listening is the effort to grasp the heart of a pastoral problem in order to respond with an appropriate pastoral solution. Both of these forms of listening remain central to effective pastoral ministry and leadership.

Because priests and bishops so often listen attentively to questions and pastoral problems brought to their rectories and chanceries, they remain convinced that they are indeed good listeners. As we shall see, there is another kind of listening that is equally important for church leaders—the ability to listen for the voice of the Spirit that often can be heard in the life and faith experiences of the faithful.[10] If church leaders, especially our bishops, really believe they have nothing to learn in terms of doctrine, morals, and the life of the spirit, except from members of the college of bishops, then the process, as Bishop Murphy observed, is indeed flawed, to say the least.

Respectful of the important role women religious play in the life of the church and ready to listen "from the heart," a number of bishops meet regularly with the leadership of the religious congregations based in their dioceses. Such meetings provide opportunities for women in leadership roles to offer counsel to the bishop in matters relating to the diocese and, where appropriate, to discuss issues or concerns relating to their congregations. In some dioceses, the council of major superiors functions as one of the primary consultative groups to which the bishop regularly turns for dialogue and advice. Of course, the level of dialogue and collaboration where such councils exist varies to a great degree on the openness and leadership style of the bishop.

Uneven though they may be in terms of process and effectiveness, these structural attempts to provide forums for the voices of women religious are welcomed for the most part by vowed religious. That they often prove frustrating and discouraging to some is due largely to the ecclesial vision of the diocesan bishop and to the structural, human, and theological limitations present in every age of the church's history. With due respect for attempts to foster dialogue between church authorities and church women, leadership and influence, that is, power, remain in the hands of male clerics, the ordained ministers of the church. As long as women are excluded from meaningful positions of leadership and continue to be barred even from ordination to the diaconate, it is difficult to see how their wisdom and insight, their vision and charisms, will be adequately brought to light in service of the gospel and the people of God.[11]

Faithful Imagination

Walter Brueggemann writes that "[i]t is abundantly and un-mistakably clear that we are in deep *dislocation* in our society that touches every aspect of our lives."[12] The dislocation, displacement, and confusion of which he speaks have profoundly touched the life of the church. Consider the realities Brueggeman lists as signs of the current crisis:

- The old certitudes are less certain.
- The old privileges are under powerful challenge.
- The old dominations are increasingly ineffective, and we seem not to be so clearly in charge.
- The old institutions (governmental, educational, judicial, medical) seem less and less to deliver what is intended and long counted upon.
- The old social fabrics of neighborliness are eroded into selfishness, fear, anger, and greed. . . .
- There is great confusion in the church about authority.
- There is bewilderment about mission, for we tend to think in triumphalist categories, even while some speak of the United States as a "mission field."
- We all know about the heavy, mean-spirited disputes about norms and ethics.[13]

These cultural realities form the social context for the ecclesial issues at the heart of the crisis facing the church and reveal the complex web of forces and dynamics at play here. No one group, either in society at large or in the church, has the resources required for prudently and effectively addressing the present challenges to church and society. The wisdom of the whole community, men and women, laity and clergy, young and old, is needed. To a significant degree, we have held our imagination in check and denied our thirst for voices of inspiration and courage by excluding women from most of the positions of spiritual and administrative leadership in the church. The task at hand is to begin breaking

through age-encrusted walls of denial and silence. The task at
hand is to listen to the voices of wisdom and faith whether spoken
by women or men. Here Brueggemann identifies the impasse and
points to a path through it. "Our bewildered, numbed, despairing
society lacks ways of thinking and ways of speaking that can give
us remedial access to the crisis, that can (1) go deep into the crisis
and so avoid *denial*, and (2) imagine past the crisis, and so avoid
despair enacted as abdicating silence (emphasis in original). It is
clear to me that the twin temptations of denial and despair are
powerfully at work to prevent any serious engagement of the crisis of dislocation into which we are now plunged."[14]

What Brueggemann and others are calling for, new ways of
speaking, new ways of knowing, and new ways of imagining, are
vital to any attempts to address the present crisis.[15] Thankfully,
there are indeed voices speaking and imagining in new ways that
inspire hope and point us beyond the impasse. Tragically, many of
these voices speak to deaf ears. These, I propose, are the voices of
women that are heard, if at all, with guarded defensiveness and
wary suspicion. It is worth repeating that much is being lost here
for many women are "speaking the truth in love" with fresh voices
and with inspired insight.[16]

Most of these voices speak to our imaginations in ways that
remind us of God's saving fidelity when the church faced crises in
the past. They are voices of hope. These same voices prompt us to
move beyond the present denial and silence to see new possibilities—possibilities that can only be realized when the fears that
breed denial and silence are named and faced. They are voices of
faith. If a major part of the present crisis facing the church is a crisis in imagination, and I believe it is, then the "faithful imagination" of all members of the church deserves to be heard with respect
and openness.[17]

Imagination, no matter how faithful, remains largely suspect
in many corridors of the church. Rather than seen as one of humanity's greatest "faculties," it is viewed with suspicion especially
by church authorities whose understanding of both doctrine and

discipline is steadfastly static. From this perspective, faithful imagination, creative thought, and promising possibilities are not only discouraged but often actively blocked out of fear for the integrity of church teaching. We saw this ecclesial attitude in full force when Pope John XXIII called for the pastoral council, Vatican II. Such fear truncates the role of the Spirit to a mission of preservation. Sadly, our history reveals, it triumphs over hope and trust more often than not. Those who embody this kind of fear believe they stand under the banner of faith in defense of faith, blind to their own impoverishment of faith. When dominant, fear not only stifles the inspiration of the Spirit, it tends to sap the church of its vitality and dynamism. At its worst, it is actually destructive as it strives to make unchanging that which is alive and fresh: generation after generation of believers bringing the light and freedom of the gospel to culture after culture, to age upon age.

In such a climate of fear, imagination and all creative energies are perceived as dangerous—and especially when they rise from the voices of women. Wherever, whenever imagination is stifled, we should know by now, religion runs the risk of becoming a museum of ritual and canonical prescriptions, often rich with meaning and significance for ages past, but impotent to speak compellingly to the hearts of men and women struggling to be faithful in an age of chaos and challenge.

It is not surprising, then, that when women's voices critique the androcentric bias of religion and theology, they regularly are met with strikingly unimaginative responses, responses that often can be reduced to simple assertions of the status quo. Heard or not, their voices will continue to speak "the truth in love." It simply cannot be otherwise. Today thousands of Catholic women have been trained in all fields of theology, and hundreds have obtained doctorates in theology and related disciplines.[18] Their work, writes Catherine Mowry LaCugna, "highlights new images and metaphors for both God and human experience, and revises the way we use theological and religious language."[19] Add to these numbers women who have studied theology at the undergraduate level and women who read widely in Catholic periodicals, and we discover a wellspring of imaginative, provocative, and faithful Catholic thought.

Not only does the faithful imagination of women look to the future, to the way things might be if we were more faithful to the teachings of Jesus and the inspiration of the Spirit, it also looks to the past, and in doing so renders a stinging critique of ecclesial attitudes and culture that have virtually silenced the voices of women. Their faithful imagination reminds us that men and women share fully in human nature, that neither is superior to the other.[20] These women call us to remember that "[n]either men nor women can claim to be closer to God or more perfectly created in God's image without vitiating the truths of the Christian faith and the authenticity of biblical revelation."[21] Like the faithful imagination of men, women's faithful imagination (especially the voices of women theologians) deserves to be taken seriously, critiqued on its merits, and when found compelling, integrated into the collective wisdom and vision of the church.

Breaking Silence

Over tea and scones Medical Missionary of Mary Sr. Maura O'Donohue, a medical doctor, spoke softly of the terrible reality that had come to her attention involving the sexual exploitation of religious sisters by priests and bishops. She spoke with a physician's precision, yet with compassion and heartfelt anguish about the abuse numerous religious, mainly in developing countries, were suffering. We sat in the living room of her sister's and brother-in-law's home in a Cleveland suburb, our meeting arranged by one of my seminary classmates who is a mutual friend. There were hints of hurt in her voice, linked both to the abuse of so many sisters she had come to know and admire and to the painful, and in some cases, mean-spirited criticism directed at her by some African clergy. The criticism, often vitriolic, welled up from well-protected denial. Her report, more of which we shall see shortly, was perceived in some quarters as an attack on the integrity of African sisters, priests, and bishops. The force of the denial and minimization was telling. Inner spaces where personal and collective images of worth and dignity are nourished had been invaded. When that happens, individuals fight for their lives, often using for weapons denial and personal vilification. Maura O'Donohue, I could see, was dealing with both.

I felt I understood the pain she was enduring in the wake of the March 16, 2001, cover story in the *National Catholic Reporter* addressing the abuse of African sisters and other nuns by clergy. The *NCR* story drew upon at least five credible sources, one of which was O'Donohue's 1994 "strictly confidential" memo to church authorities on the abuse of vowed religious women, many in formation, by priests and bishops. While not excluding similar abuses by clergy in more than two dozen countries, O'Donohue's report (apparently in private circulation for a number of years) and the *NCR* cover story called attention to the widespread cries for help coming from African sisters she had come to know while serving as AIDS coordinator for the Catholic Fund for Overseas Development based in England. The assignment included numerous visits to many countries in Africa (as well as Asia, the Americas, and Europe) during which she learned that numerous priests and bishops, fearful of contracting the AIDS virus from women of the cities and villages, turned to religious sisters as safe outlets for their sexual desires.

The episodes, brought to her attention with urgent pleadings for help, revealed a consistent, almost incomprehensible pattern to the behaviors. It was clear that the abuse was more than incidental. Supporting O'Donohue's report, Abbot Nokter Wolf, abbot primate of the Benedictine order, stated in an interview with the *National Catholic Reporter*, "I don't believe these are simply exceptional cases. I think the abuse described is happening. How much it happens, what the numbers are, I have no way of knowing. But it is a serious matter, and we need to discuss it."[22]

O'Donohue's memo was but one of numerous voices raised in an effort to alleviate the suffering of large numbers of African sisters. In November 1998, Missionaries of Our Lady of Africa sister Marie McDonald presented a paper, titled "The Problem of the Sexual Abuse of African Religious in Africa and Rome," to the Council of 16 (delegates from the Union of Superiors General, an association representing men's religious communities based in Rome; the International Union of Superiors General, an organization representing women religious; and the Vatican Congregation for Institutes of Consecrated Life and Societies of Apostolic Life). And addressing a September 2000 Rome congress of 250 Benedictine abbots, Benedictine sister Esther Fangman, raised the same issue.[23]

The reality of the abuse, first raised by O'Donohue in 1994, and acknowledged in a March 20, 2001, public statement by Vatican spokesperson, Dr. Joaquin Navarro-Valls, was, as noted above, the subject of a cover story in the March 16, 2001, issue of the *National Catholic Reporter*. I mention it here because of the silence, and in some cases denial, with which it was met. While it is true that Cardinal Eduardo Martinez, prefect of the Congregation for Religious and Secular Institutes, met with O'Donohue in February 1995 to hear first hand of her report, the matter was addressed by bringing it to the attention of bishops in whose dioceses the abuse was taking place and other appropriate ecclesial bodies. In some cases, however, the diocesan bishop asked to address the matter was himself one of the abusers.

In her meeting with Cardinal Martinez, O'Donohue had proposed the appointment of an Apostolic Visitator to investigate the issues brought to light in her report, believing that, "Such a visitation on a low key basis would give enormous encouragement to local religious who have pleaded with us to bring these matters directly to the attention of the Holy See. It would be seen as a potent sign of pre-occupation and solicitous care for those same religious."[24]

The behaviors reported by O'Donohue, McDonald, and others proved, to no one's surprise, profoundly disturbing and scandalous. And the church responded—if slowly and cautiously. In November 2001, the Council of 16 announced guidelines and procedures aimed at curtailing the sexual exploitation of sisters. McDonald's and O'Donohue's reports at last had led to corrective action on the part of the church.[25] Whether the response was appropriate is best left for others to decide; it is clearly too early to measure its effectiveness. The question remains, however, whether the abusive behaviors would have received even the attention and corrective action they did if O'Donohue's and McDonald's confidential reports had not been brought to the attention of the media.

In most cases, I believe, silence, denial, and minimization occur out of concern for the perceived harm church authorities feel would follow upon negative, scandalous reports of clergy misconduct. We still haven't learned as a church that secrecy and denial only tend to exacerbate the harmful effects of inappropriate and scandalous behaviors. Certainly, the scandalous behaviors of church personnel when brought to the light of public attention cast a shadow over the committed and faithful work of most priests and bishops, most religious and lay pastoral ministers. We have, as a church, failed to understand that we insult the intelligence of parishioners and people in general when we believe they cannot distinguish between the two.[26]

The disclosure of abuse of sisters in Africa and other countries by clergy, the widespread sexual abuse of minors by priests and bishops, and reports of large numbers of priests dying of AIDS are regularly "contextualized" by some church authorities out of fear that they will weaken the long-standing discipline of obligatory celibacy. In an editorial titled "A Scandal to Face Together," reflecting on the reports of O'Donohue and McDonald, *The Tablet* observed, "The Catholic discipline of obligatory celibacy took a further knock this week with the publication of shocking details of sexual abuse of nuns by clergy. Such accounts are often hearsay, but in this case there can be no gainsaying the authority of the authors. . . ."[27] Fearing precisely such dents in celibacy's armor, church officials can be seen assuming the role of "spin doctors" attempting to frame these issues as symptoms of human weakness quite unrelated to historically conditioned structures that beg for discussion and review. The same editorial continued:

Africans are highly sensitive to any criticism that might imply that their young Churches are failing, and the Vatican has had to tread warily. Even allowing for the necessary delicacy, however, it is clear that the courteous and restrained representations made by these leading women religious have not been treated with anything like the urgency they deserved. Worse than that: one can hardly believe our special correspondent's statement that a mother general in Malawi was publicly removed from her post by her archbishop after she reported to him that 29 nuns in her community had been made pregnant by priests. But the fact is well documented.

At stake here is a basic respect for women in the Church and an absolute duty of bishops to support them. Our special correspondent notes that at last the women themselves are taking steps. In the words of Sr. Marie McDonald, there is "a conspiracy of silence surrounding this issue. Only if we can look at it honestly will we be able to find solutions."[28]

Both Maura O'Donohue and Marie McDonald have suffered stinging criticism for their confidential reports to appropriate church authorities about the abuse of their sisters by priests. They have been accused of betraying the very people they attempted to save from abuse. In an essay critical of O'Donohue, McDonald, and the *National Catholic Reporter*, a Jesuit from Zambia studying at the Jesuit School of Theology at Berkeley, California, writes:

The African nuns have been depicted being naïve, stupid, poor and miserable victims. Even if we were to admit that some sisters may have been made pregnant by some priests, it is unforgivable to submit to the sin of silence in the face of such callous attacks on women of dignity and honor striving to serve their people in sacrifice and commitment. Local congregations are doing well and producing sisters of quality. If the article [by John L. Allen, Jr. and Pamela Schaeffer, *NCR*, March 16, 2001] intended to be an advocate for the African woman, it has erred: It actually has dragged the dignity of an African woman into the mud. Advocacy for the empowerment of African women cannot be achieved by insulting them.[29]

Whether applauded or criticized, whether heeded or dismissed, women continue to express their souls' deepest longings. A few of their voices are shrill and some expose smoldering embers of anger, even rage. Most, however, are intelligent, loving, and faithful voices calling the church to listen more urgently to the promptings of the Spirit. With considerable courage, they speak the truth in love from Africa, Asia, Europe, and the Americas, indeed, from every corner of the world. If we listen carefully, nondefensively, we will hear more than the words they speak—we will hear silent cords of hope and fidelity, of wisdom and compassion. We will hear in the spirit and conviction out of which they speak that which cannot be spoken—their enduring, radical trust in the One whose image they have been created.

CHAPTER FIVE

RELIGIOUS LIFE AND THE PRIESTHOOD

Man [and woman] cannot stand to lead a meaningless life.

—C. G. Jung

No one (at least no one in her right mind) undertakes this prophetic vocation on her own initiative. It is a response to a call, mysterious in its origin and its manifestation. It is finally a response of love to Love, and that is more than sufficient to account for its totality and permanence, even in a world of fragmented commitments and hedged bets.

—Sandra M. Schneiders, I.H.M., *Finding the Treasure*

The institutional forms of priesthood, as we have known them over the past several hundred years, are moving toward death.

—James D. Whitehead

YEARS AGO WHEN I WAS TEACHING at Ursuline College in Ohio, four nursing students in my abnormal psychology class, all good friends, stood out from their peers. Clearly blessed with engaging personalities and an unselfconscious wholesomeness, they regularly appeared for weekday Mass as well as Sunday Eucharist. They were also active participants in retreats and other activities sponsored by the college's campus ministry. Because I served as a part-time campus minister in addition to my teaching responsibilities, our paths crossed often and soon I came to know these young women rather well. They were both fun-loving and mature for

their years. Through casual conversations and more serious dialogues, I came to see their commitment to leading gospel-based
lives of service and simplicity. During one of these conversations,
I asked them if they had ever thought of religious life, mention-
ing that it was clear to me that each of them took their spiritual
lives seriously and that they approached their future nursing roles
as a kind of ministry. The conversation and their response have
stayed with me over the years.

Without a moment's hesitation, they smiled and shook their
heads. No, they said, they had never seriously thought of religious
life. But they went on to tell me of their plans after graduation.
They wanted to find work at the same hospital, if possible, and
they wanted to rent a home together and share the expenses. They
hoped there would be time each day for common prayer and, if all
went as planned, they would join the local parish and be as active
as their work schedules would permit. When I told them their plan
sounded rather like religious life to me, they nodded. But, they
added, we want the freedom to be open to dating and possible marriage. While they desired to work in a healing profession and lead
a common life grounded in prayer and friendship—indeed a kind
of religious life—they gave little if any serious thought to entering a novitiate.

They are all married now, and mothers. They never expected
their noble commitment to a common life rooted in the gospel to
last for more than a few years. And it didn't. Now, decades later, I
think of these four good and generous women with considerable
fondness. When people ask where have all the vocations gone,
they come to mind.

These women, and others like them, may be telling us something as we witness the dramatic drop in the number of young
(and not so young) people entering religious life and our seminaries. I believe there are countless Catholics who desire to make a
difference with their lives, who know already what really matters,
and who are open to God's plan for them. The goodness, idealism,
and courage are there. The faith is there. Yet, for the most part,

they are not drawn to our convents and seminaries. And, for the most part, we don't ask why. We do ask God to "send us more vocations." The prayer unnerves me. God really isn't holding out on us. We do ask parents, priests, brothers, and sisters to more actively recruit potential candidates for religious life and the priesthood. But we don't ask if the present structures defining the lived experience of religious life and priesthood need rethinking and renewal. And all the while the signs point to the need for "new wineskins."[1] But this would lead to disturbing questions and to thorny issues—mandatory celibacy, for example, concerning the priesthood, and lifetime commitment, for example, concerning religious life. And so, for the most part, we keep silent, refusing to take the hard look the vocation crisis calls for.

Thankfully, there are exceptions. Most notable among them is the current multivolume work of Sandra Schneiders, *Finding the Treasure: Locating Catholic Religious Life in a New Ecclesial and Cultural Context* and *Selling All: Commitment, Consecrated Celibacy, and Community in Catholic Religious Life.*[2] Both of Schneiders' published books in this series have received early acclaim—and rightly so. She addresses all the relevant issues—cultural context, celibacy, permanent commitment, formation, community—with balance and insight. What Schneiders has done and continues to do for religious life needs to be done for the priesthood in these first years of the new millennium. A deeply ingrained and pervasive fear, I am afraid, will keep us from moving anytime soon in this direction. The origins and nature of this fear will be addressed later in this chapter as well as in succeeding chapters.

The Collapse of Convent Culture

In his masterful work, *American Catholic*, Charles R. Morris marks the extraordinary contribution religious sisters made to the vitality and success of Catholic life and culture and to the overall success of Catholics in the first centuries of the church's life in the new world:

The nuns were the system's faceless heroes. They tended the altars and staffed the institutions—the schools, the hospitals—required by a separatist Catholic state. A nun's life was highly restricted—even visits home were rare—and pay was low, only $300 a year for an elementary schoolteacher, paid to the order, not to the nun. Nuns were not entirely without psychic income: adults treated them with exaggerated respect, and they were held in awe by schoolchildren. But they were often badly overworked. . . . Still convents were turning away an onslaught of applicants, a comment, perhaps, on the power of faith, but also on the bleak prospects facing so many working-class girls of the time.[3]

Living, for the most part, in convents, they led a common life of considerable mystery and selfless service that rivaled the mystery and respect priests enjoyed until the middle of the 1980s. Their competence, discipline, and energy, not to mention their readiness to work, for all practical purposes, for room and board, guaranteed the unparalleled success of American Catholic schools, especially on the parish level. Their work in hospitals and social service agencies was equally distinguished. For decades, especially the middle decades of the twentieth century, this religious culture of simple, communal living and meaningful ministry in schools, hospitals, and social service agencies captured the imaginations of thousands of young Catholic women.

Deborah Kerr in the 1957 film, *Heaven Knows, Mr. Allison*, portrayed the idealized nun to the hilt: modest, attractive, intelligent, and devout. Robert Mitchum, playing the worldly, tough-minded Marine Corporal Allison, found himself falling in love, fascinated by the innocence and measured reserve of Kerr's Sister Angela. The nonbelieving Mr. Allison was captivated by her mysterious peace of soul. And so were countless Catholics.[4] While many would confess to not understanding the nature and everyday world of religious life, there was indeed something about it that had the power to capture one's imagination. Motherhouses were built or expanded to meet the needs of a steady stream of women, most from working and middle-class families, seeking admission. And then, in what appeared to be a blink of an eye, the number of applicants dropped dramatically. A generation ago, the number of U.S. vowed religious women totaled approximately 200,000. In the year 2000, the number was down to an alarming 77,844, a steeper decline than the drop in seminarians and priests during the same period. In the 1940s, Charles Morris reports the Archdiocese of Philadelphia enjoyed a 5:1 ratio of nuns to priests.[5] Today, the ratio of nuns to priests is roughly 2:1.[6] In many congregations of sisters, the average age of the members is seventy or higher, and in some it approaches eighty. Reflecting on the aging of the American sister, Morris writes, "Each time I met a young, native-born American woman who was a nun, like Diane Steele, a graduate theology student at Notre Dame, or Laura Reicks at the USCC [United States Catholic Conference], it registered as a major event."[7] In many congregations today, the youngest sisters are in their fifties.

As the number of sisters declined, so did life in the convent.[8] Today's sisters, as likely to be working as diocesan administrators, professors, lawyers, physicians, and hospital executives as teachers in parish schools, are choosing to live in rented homes, apartments, or condominiums. And many are living alone. In one congregation I know of, more than half of the sisters are living by themselves. The congregation's leaders report that the sisters' morale and sense of identity are holding strong. But, it is reasonable to ask, for how long? Two perspectives hold forth. One believes that women's religious life will rebound with renewed structures and a fresh understanding of its essence and mission appropriate for the new millennium.[9] The other believes that the end is likely near. "If the demographics of the priesthood are daunting, the future of female religious orders is probably hopeless," states Charles R. Morris.[10]

There is a certain realism to the latter position. We have known for some time now that the birth rate for Catholic families in the U.S. is less than two children (1.85), the same rate for families in general.[11] It is likely, then, that many Catholic parents will have but one daughter. Parental support, let alone encouragement, for a daughter considering religious life is likely to be weak.

This downsizing of the Catholic family is also a factor in the diminishing number of seminarians, an issue to which we will turn later in this chapter.[12] And when we factor in the Vatican Council's positive evaluation of human sexuality which reinforced in turn our understanding of marriage as a true vocation, a true call to holiness, the religious vocation picture does indeed seem dark.[13]

My own hunch is that the major, international orders, such as the Benedictines and Sisters of Notre Dame, will survive. And it is likely that many federations of religious congregations will also. Unfortunately, the factors mentioned here support Morris' assessment, especially for the small, diocesan congregations of sisters. I remain particularly hopeful, nonetheless, for contemplative congregations of nuns—not only because they appear to be holding their own for the most part as apostolic communities suffer shrinking numbers and the aging of their sisters, but because of the present cultural crisis in American society. In the midst of our relentless consumerist society, a society that places more value on things than on relationships, on possessions rather than on wisdom and a sense of meaning and purpose, a number of spiritually sensitive women and men will seek out viable alternatives. These individuals will be among the first to awaken to the disillusionment, deadening self-centeredness, and inner emptiness such consumerist cultures inevitably foster. Some will seek the radically different path of contemplative community life grounded in gospel simplicity and poverty.[14]

My four young friends from Ursuline College may have been hedging their bets when they chose to lead a common life that placed prayer and service at the center of things without making a permanent commitment to it. But I rather doubt it. Their discernment was honest and real—they listened for the voice of the Spirit and trusted their intuition as faithful women of prayer. Each believed correctly that she had a calling to live the Christian life as fully as she could. That their understanding of this calling did not lead them to formal religious life, I believe, is significant. The possibility of entering "the convent," to use an image from computer technology, wasn't even on the screen. It's clear to me that we need to listen to individuals like these young nurses. They have much to say about the present categories and structures of religious life. Perhaps, had they not eventually separated in order to marry, they may have been surprised to find their lifestyle attracting other young women who shared their faith and vision. Especially when specific social needs go unmet, small numbers of like-minded Christians attempting to address them may evolve into small "religious" communities, the very genesis of most apostolic congregations in past centuries. Even in this crisis period, new forms of religious life may well be germinating.

Facing the Present Reality

While there is clearly some denial among the sisters of relatively small, diocesan congregations and among some whose numbers for the present are declining at more modest rates, it appears to be the exception. The church can learn a great deal here. Most congregations, however, are willing to look at their situations courageously and honestly. Their superiors and leadership councils continue to consider the options available to them, plan intelligently for downsizing and possible mergers, and speak to their sisters with candor and compassion about the realities they must face. Some communities I am familiar with wisely recount their stories of origin and note the obstacles, challenges, failures, and successes that make up their history. Celebrating their history and the ministerial needs that brought most of them into existence, they are prepared to acknowledge that, like individual organisms, religious communities also have life-spans.

Decline and extinction are not necessarily signs of failure; the congregation's mission for a given time and place may simply be completed.[15] Aware of the historical reality that most religious congregations of women and men known to the church are no longer in existence, their leaders recognize that, in addition to planning for the immediate needs of the community, especially for the care of the elderly and infirm, they have considerable grief work to do, both personally and collectively. One of the negative effects of denial, not surprisingly, is the spiritual and psychological harm done to the individual and community when the need for grieving remains unacknowledged.[16] To their credit, religious communities of women appear ready to honor this human need.

The basic thrust and vitality of religious life in the new millennium may well be determined in a decade or two. How some congregations may flourish, how others survive, and how, in many cases, they die, will prove profoundly instructive, I suspect, to the whole church.

Lay Ecclesial Ministry and the Diaconate

Before taking stock of the alarming demographics relating to priests and seminarians, it is important to note what theologian Thomas O'Meara has described as an explosion of vocations to fulltime parochial ministry that has grown in a direct inverse correlation to the drop in seminary vocations during the last decades of the twentieth century.[17] Comprised mostly of women, (approximately 54 percent lay, 28 percent vowed religious, and 17 percent lay men) an expanding corps of some thirty thousand lay ministers is filling parish staffing needs exacerbated by the precipitous drop in the ranks of the priesthood.[18] Ministering alongside priests and deacons, these ministers bear witness to a phenomenon rarely seen in the church's history—large numbers of the laity discerning a call to live out their baptismal vocation as ecclesial ministers.

These women and men, working for salaries that often compare quite poorly to the broader work world, are meeting pastoral needs—ministry to the ill and homebound, religious education and sacramental formation, as well as a myriad of other parish services—that would otherwise go unmet or severely stretch the pastor's resources. They differ from lay ministers who give a year or so after college in the various volunteer programs sponsored by churches, universities, and government programs since they usually commit to ongoing service at a specific parish and bring to their ministry both formal and informal ministerial training. In some cases, after course work and formation that approaches the first years of seminary programs, they are certified by the local church as lay ecclesial ministers. In not a few dioceses, lay ecclesial ministers are joining the growing number of deacons and religious who serve as parish administrators in the absence of resident priests.

This vocational phenomenon deserves serious theological reflection. How successfully do these new ministers minister? How does their training vary from diocese to diocese? How are they received by their ordained co-ministers? How are they received by the parishioners they serve? And finally, would some or even many of these lay ministers consider religious life if a temporary commitment were available or the priesthood if obligatory celibacy were dropped? Such questions, of course, take us into dangerous waters. An editorial in a Catholic newspaper summarized the danger:

> Particularly troubling is the suspicion that the shepherds are silent in the face of the crisis [shortage of priests] not because they lack the imagination or insight to articulate a vision but because they fear the consequences of giving voice to their ideas. They fear the consequences of tapping the imaginations and expertise of well-trained priests and laity in their midst.
>
> The fear is understandable. Under the current administration in Rome, such discussions are forbidden. Our current bishops know what has happened to the careers of those who have gone before them and who have dared to dream new dreams.[19]

Still, the questions deserve to be asked. And the answers that surface deserve serious reflection.

Some of these questions could serve as an introduction to a theological reflection on the role and relatively brief history of the permanent diaconate. Approximately half of the U.S. dioceses draw upon this long-neglected hierarchical ministry that was re-claimed by the council fathers. In spite of reports that diaconal ministry is generally effective and well received, at least in many if not all of the dioceses where deacons function, the jury may still be out on the overall feasibility of the permanent diaconate based on the decision of a number of bishops to suspend their formation programs for deacons.

Nonetheless, candidates for the diaconate continue to come forward. Many are exceptional men of faith—intelligent, compe-tent, generous, and mature. Others may prove, like some priests, laity, and religious, to do more harm than good. Screening, ad-mission standards, and training, understandably enough, vary from diocese to diocese. Deacons, of course, can be married men. Should a deacon's wife die, however, the deacon is not permitted by canon law to remarry without giving up his ministry as dea-con! How many, one wonders, would consider ministry as priests if they were allowed to marry?

The Dramatic Drop in the Number of Priests

So well known is the dramatic and alarming drop in the num-ber of priests and seminarians that it is tedious for many Catho-lics to hear the statistics that lay bare the crisis. Nonetheless, a brief summary may be helpful. While the U.S. Catholic popula-tion continues to grow (the number of registered Catholics in 1999 was 60.3 million, compared to 28.6 million in the 1950s and likely as high as 67 million in 2001 when nonregistered Catholics are factored in), researchers project a 40 percent drop in the num-ber of active diocesan priests in the period between 1965 and 2005.[20] A look at the last decade of the twentieth century reflects a relentless downward trend. In 1990 there were 24,603 active diocesan priests; in 2000 there were 20,131; and researchers pro-ject only 18,197 in the year 2006.[21] From another perspective, the ratio of Catholics to priests, 1,000 to 1, just a few decades ago, is now calculated to be 2,200 to 1.[22]

But within the staggering drop in numbers of priests is yet more disturbing news. Only 6 percent of U.S. priests are thirty-five years-of-age and younger.[23] A recent study directed by Dean Hoge of Catholic University reports that 10 to 15 percent of priests ordained five years or less resigned from active ministry, up from an estimated 8 to 10 percent in the 1980s.[24] The major reason cited for their resignations was the isolation and loneliness of celibacy. Not only, then, do we have a major drop in the number of priests thirty-five and under, one in seven priests ordained five years or less is resigning. In a national presbyterate with an average age of almost sixty and climbing, the number of priests over ninety may soon be larger than the number of priests under thirty-five. A senior Diocese of Brooklyn priest reports, "In one large city diocese, the number of priests over seventy-one—the retirement age—is five times the number of priests who are under forty."[25]

The picture painted by seminary enrollments is hardly encouraging. Excluding undergraduate candidates for the priesthood, diocesan seminarians in 1997 numbered 2,268, down from 4,761 in 1968.[26] Like their counterparts in Protestant seminaries, they tend to be considerably older than seminarians of past generations, averaging in the low to mid-thirty range.[27] Most have considerable work and life experience—priesthood may be their second or even third career—and some have been married. Indeed, some are parents and grandparents. Such older candidates often encounter formation programs historically geared to much younger aspirants. After many years of living in their own home, condo, or apartment, the adjustment to seminary life can be challenging. Like many of the younger seminarians in their early twenties, these older candidates may struggle with issues of maturity and sexual identity.[28] It is clear, however, that without these second and third career candidates, the vocation crisis would be much worse than it is.

From time to time, we still hear one bishop or another denying any kind of vocation crisis or need for alarm about the present demographics shaping the contemporary priesthood. I believe they feel any kind of acknowledgment of the current reality will foster a kind of negativism that will only make the situation worse. The same anxiety, moreover, can be detected at the highest levels of the church. Paul Philibert writes, "[S]tatistical accounting for the demographics of ordained leadership in the universal Church has become a matter of great political sensitivity. Vatican congregations are clearly reluctant to accept that a sea change is taking place in the demographics of ministry worldwide."[29] Consider, for example, the July 31, 1996, essay in *L'Osservatore Romano*, the Vatican's quasi-official newspaper, claiming a 75 percent increase in seminarians and priests worldwide between the years 1975 and 1995. By way of contrast, the Official Catholic Directory for the U.S. reported that while U.S. Catholics grew by nearly one million in 1996, there were 974 fewer priests and 1,481 fewer nuns compared to the previous year. While there are indeed relatively large numbers of candidates for the priesthood and religious life in a number of Asian, African, and Eastern Europe countries, missionaries and seminary personnel from these same countries report high drop-out rates. The situation in Europe and North America, however, remains critical. As noted earlier in this chapter, church officials continue to call for more effective and active recruiting and for increased prayers for vocations. The question remains—what else might we expect from our church leaders?

One answer to this question comes from Fr. James E. Sullivan, director *emeritus* of the Religious Consultation Center of the Diocese of Brooklyn. In a candid and direct essay on the shortage of priests in the December 2001 issue of *U.S. Catholic*, Sullivan sees priestly morale being affected by the crisis in numbers and with obvious concern for his brother priests, writes, "[T]he morale of priests has . . . reached a new low. And they are most discouraged by the fact that the hierarchy of the Church does not seem to be facing the problem with openness and honesty. Priests wonder, 'What could possibly be the reason for this conspiracy of silence?'"[30] At the core of the conspiracy of silence, Sullivan believes, is the law of mandatory celibacy. "This conspiracy of silence, of course, comes directly from the Vatican, which has put a ban on all discussion of celibacy as the cause of the vocation crisis. And the U.S. bishops, out of loyalty to the pope, have strictly enforced that ban, leaving their priests and their people unbelievably frustrated and wondering how any problem can be solved if one cannot investigate what causes it."[31] Sullivan, writing with considerable passion, wants to be fair. He immediately adds:

> In fairness to the Vatican, I feel sure that there is no lack of sincerity on the part of the pope or his curia. They understand that the desire for marriage and family is such a powerful force in our human nature that they dare not open the door to honest discussion of celibacy for fear there would be an overwhelming demand for a change in that discipline. But a problem is never solved by pretending it doesn't exist.[32]

Sullivan's analysis, I believe, is accurate. Not long after *The Changing Face of the Priesthood* was released in February 2000, I had an opportunity to speak with a Vatican archbishop. He told me that he had read the book—and liked it. Then, he added, "They are reading it at the Vatican." Whether he meant in his own congregation or throughout the Vatican remains unclear. "They think you want optional celibacy," he continued. "What I want," I said, "is honest discussion about the many issues facing the priesthood today." The archbishop seemed relieved.

The factors behind the vocation crisis—which include mandatory celibacy—are, without question, complex. We need, nevertheless, to do our best to name them, study them carefully, and remain steadfastly open to where they may point us. The analysis which follows may be helpful in our collective efforts to understand the causes leading to the sharp decline in the numbers of candidates for the priesthood and religious life. At least I hope it will engage us in honest discussion.

The Vocation Crisis

For centuries now priests and religious have encouraged young men and women to search their hearts for what we have come to understand in Catholic circles as a "vocation." Vocation, it was understood, was a calling from God to a brave, joyful commitment to service as a priest, brother, sister, or, in more recent years, as deacon. Furthermore, it was a sign of preferment—the young man or woman was chosen by God (while others were not) for a special place in the life and mission of the church. A vocation in this sense merited social regard and even reverence from most Catholics.

Of course, we understand vocation in a broader sense since the council called by Pope John XXIII. The call to discipleship as a follower of Christ in the waters of baptism is the primary vocation of all the Christian faithful. Our common vocation is to be transformed again and again by the power of the Spirit into a people of faith, hope, and love. At its root, this common vocation is a call to holiness as disciples of Christ. We make concrete this common vocation by discerning the particular path that appears to be God's plan for us. Thus, it may be said that we each have "vocations" that in God's mysterious ways are intended to further the reign of God in history and lead to our ultimate salvation—a life in communion with God and God's saints.

Some of these vocational paths carry the dignity of sacrament—priesthood, diaconate, and marriage. Others, especially from the Middle Ages on, have assumed a hierarchy of dignity and status. Following the sacramental vocations to priesthood (I include the episcopacy in the priesthood category) and diaconate, the ranking, from the top down, goes something like this: virgins, especially virgin martyrs; vowed religious, especially cloistered, contemplative religious; those called to marriage even though marriage has been formally recognized as a sacrament from the beginning of the thirteenth century; and finally single people, especially if the single state appears to be God's plan for an individual and not just the absence of the opportunity to marry. As we can see, virginity and celibacy surface as the essential features for the more exalted stations on the vocational hierarchy.[33]

There are signs, however, that the church is beginning to recognize the implications of linking vocational status and holiness to the absence of an active sexual life. John Paul II's beatification of Luigi and Maria Quattrocchi in the waning days of 2001 was a first for a married couple. The Quattrocchis were married for forty-six years and had four children, three of whom discerned vocations to religious life. The fourth child remained single. Still, it should be noted, the couple gave up sexual relations "at the suggestion of their spiritual advisor" when Luigi was forty-six and Maria forty-one.[34]

In spite of these developments in our understanding of the universal call to holiness and discipleship, "vocation" in the Catholic imagination continues to signal a "higher calling" to the priesthood and/or religious life. Notice the graphics on prayer cards for vocations. Images of priests, sisters, brothers, and deacons are likely to be seen. Still, the council's teaching on the common vocation to holiness appears to be slowly undermining the Catholic imagination's notion of what holiness is all about and this in turn is apparently affecting the life decisions of many of our young women and men.

Focusing as we are here on vocations to priesthood and religious life, what factors, we might ask, are common to the discernment process? Before my attempt to answer this question, it should be clear to the person of faith that there will always be a certain anxiety, a certain doubt about the apparent path God has in mind for an individual. Thomas Merton captured this spiritual and existential anxiety in his theologically astute vocation prayer:

My Lord God, I have no idea where I am going. I do not see the road ahead of me. I cannot know for certain where it will end. Nor do I really know myself, and the fact that I think I am following Your will does not mean that I am actually doing so. But I believe that the desire to please You does in fact please You. And I hope I have that desire in all that I am doing. I hope that I will never do anything apart from that desire. And I know that, if I do this, You will lead me by the right road, though I may know nothing about it. Therefore I will trust You always though I may seem to be lost and in the shadow of death. I will not fear, for You are ever with me, and You will never leave me to face my perils alone.[35]

There is a dimension of mystery, then, to even the most comprehensive understanding of vocation; for all authentic ways of living out the fundamental call to an authentic life of belief, praise, and service are grounded in God's grace. We dare not make a commodity of grace or claim any certain possession of it. That being said, I would like to propose three factors, or qualities of soul, that from a human perspective signal the probability of a vocation to the priesthood and religious life: temperament, aptitude, and altruism. These elements of discernment will vary somewhat depending on whether the perceived calling is to the pastoral/apostolic life or to the monastic/contemplative life.[36]

Temperament. Assuming the presence of faith, hope, and charity and adequate interpersonal skills supported by at least a minimal level of psycho-sexuality maturity, individuals discerning a religious vocation (I include priesthood in this term) ought to possess that quality of personality that, from a psychological perspective, suit them to religious life. Here I am speaking of a fundamental openness to people, a disposition to compassion and justice, to service and, perhaps most important, a capacity for healthy, non-self-absorbing introspection and contemplation. Certainly there are numerous temperaments suited to a "religious vocation"; I simply propose here that there are temperaments that are ill-suited.

Aptitude. Individuals contemplating a religious vocation should carry at least the human potential for a lively and creative intellectual life. This is especially critical for the ministry of preaching that is central to the priesthood and to the charisms of a number of religious orders. It is also essential for the ministries of counseling and spiritual direction. Another aptitude regularly overlooked by individuals discerning a vocation and by those doing the initial screening, especially for vocations requiring pastoral work, is the potential for leadership. Preachers, pastors, religious educators, catechists, and social justice activists are *de facto* leaders. Those who inspire, instruct, challenge, and provide vision and hope exercise Christian leadership. A sign of a religious vocation, then, is the capacity or potential for leadership.

Also important for the individual discerning a religious vocation is an aptitude for community. The story is told of a group of Buddhist and Christian monks who were asked, from a human perspective, what was the most gratifying aspect of their lives. They answered almost to the man: the common life with our brothers. They were then asked what was the most difficult aspect of monastic life. The answer, not surprisingly, was the same: the common life with our brothers. If there is a cross in living alone, there is clearly a cross to be carried in living among others.

Yet without the purifying and often vexing interaction of community life, whether the community is one of shared living or shared ministry, the interior life becomes especially susceptible to dangerous aberrations. An important vocational factor, then, even for the diocesan seminarian and priest, is the aptitude for the common life. My experience has been that even for priests and religious who find themselves living alone, the healthiest of these men and women would be a grace to a community of believers. Finally, is there a capacity for sustained commitment and delayed gratification—for the perseverance required of any noble effort on behalf of the gospel? Does the candidate or potential candidate, in other words, have the capacity to "go the distance," to risk all by choosing a path not even considered by the vast majority of his or her contemporaries?

Altruism. The third factor in the discerning of a religious vocation is altruism—a capacity for transcending self-interest in the service of the gospel. It is grounded in the life through death paradox taught by Jesus of Nazareth and it presupposes a vision for a renewed church and even for a renewed social order. For both church and society are "becoming," moving by grace to reveal the reign of God in our midst. And it includes a passion for meaningful living found in the core truths of the gospel: the fullness of life follows the surrender of one's life to something bigger than oneself; God's manifest love for the poor and the least among us; the richness of soul found in detachment and spiritual poverty; the presence of grace in life's darkest moments. In other words, authentic religious vocations are sustained by a maturing faith and an abiding hope. Closely allied to altruism is its distant cousin, *idealism*. Individuals who want to make a difference with their lives, to a greater or lesser extent, are idealists. Although mocked by both secular and ecclesial cynics, their innocence and idealism remain important, even essential, to the mission of the church. The idealism of which I speak here should not be confused with perfectionism.[37] Idealism rooted in faith simply takes the saving and renewing power of grace seriously. Still, idealism has its shadow side—a subtle need for control that regularly meets frustration as people assert their rightful need for freedom and independence. Respecting the possible perversion of idealism and altruism, and the potential misreading of temperament and aptitude, these factors remain benchmarks of the call to priesthood and religious life.

To Be Set Apart

"Just a few good men." The widely recognized Marine recruiting slogan openly appeals to the human need to be noticed, to be set apart. It has interesting parallels with the recruiting strategies employed by some dioceses and religious congregations. This in itself is problematic. Both as Americans and now as post-conciliar Catholics, we are suspicious of elites of any kind. We who live in western egalitarian societies are wary of those who wish to be noticed, even acclaimed, for their station in life. We even are wary (and uncomfortable) if someone in our company expresses a desire to become holy or to be a saint. Yet there is something human and natural in this desire for self-definition and for underscoring one's unique existence. The very decision to become a priest or religious is shaped and energized precisely from this desire, often unarticulated to even family and friends, to achieve true holiness of life.

In generations past as well as in many Catholic communities today, the desire to follow a religious vocation carried with it, as we noted above, great social capital. It signaled that one of their own was serious about pursing sanctity of life, was apparently called by God to this pursuit, and thus was "exalted and apart." Consider the opening paragraph to novelist Mary Gordon's extended essay on nuns as an endangered species:

> For the whole of what I would call my childhood I wanted to be a nun. In my box of treasures, alongside my Dale Evans cowgirl outfit and my cutouts of Grace Kelly, I kept my favorite book, *The Nuns Who Hurried,* and my favorite doll, a stiff, coiffed figure in a habit of black silk. I enjoyed my cowgirl outfit and my cutouts very much, but the nun doll and the nun book had a special shimmer. They made me feel exalted and apart.[38]

We still don't know quite what to do with this natural desire to feel exalted and set apart. Can it indeed be of God? Is it compatible with authentic humility? Has its diminution in the closing decades of the twentieth century influenced the vocational choices of countless women and men—with the appropriate temperaments, aptitudes, and altruism—to exclude the possibility of pursuing a religious vocation?

Perhaps the trouble lies with the notion that to be set apart is to be "set above." A more horizontal reading allows for the understanding that one called to a religious vocation is set apart in the sense of living on the margins of society so that he or she may speak prophetically by word and example. In societies such as our own dominated by the corporate mindset, individuals are needed who move to the margins, who are set apart, in order to announce a different way of living.[39] With this understanding of being set apart, then, one assumes a position on the margins of society so as to be of service to others and a witness to others of the saving truth of the gospel. One is set apart only to find one's place at the very heart, the very center of what matters most.

We are indeed, as members of God's people, called to holiness—each and every one of us. As sons and daughters of God, as God's beloved, we stand exalted. And if some are by God's mysterious design set apart for prophetic witness, it is only to see more clearly that they are members, equal members, in the household of God. We are just now coming to see that the vocation question is profoundly communal by nature and that the subjective dimension has assumed in recent centuries an unhealthy prominence. This is clearly a healthy development. Still, we have yet to fully explore the psychological and theological implications of the universal call to holiness on the present steep decline in vocations to priesthood and religious life.

The Modern World

Another important effect of Vatican II has been a deeper understanding and appreciation of the believer's fundamental relationship with the modern world—and that it is good. The world, wounded as it is by human greed, envy, and violence, is nonetheless our home. It is the place where grace dwells and should no longer be perceived as our enemy. Throughout the conciliar documents and especially in the Pastoral Constitution on the Church in the Modern World, Catholics discovered that they too were citizens of the earth with a responsibility to be stewards of its well-being. Of course we acknowledge that we will never be completely at home here since our final destiny is to dwell with the triune God in God's household—the communion of saints. This fundamental shift, however, in the church's attitude toward the world has significantly reshaped and refocused the very process of vocation discernment. The extent and ultimate effects of this reshaping and refocusing have been assessed for some time now. As Sandra Schneiders notes:

> The ecclesial change [the Church's solidarity with the modern world] and its implications for Religious Life have been on the front

burner of our consciousness for several decades. Essentially, the Council reversed the Church's unqualified rejection of modernity, declaring its solidarity with the world and its peoples. If Church and world were now understood as mutually penetrating realities, Religious Life must also be understood as in, with, and for the world. This change constituted a Copernican revolution for Religious who had, for centuries, defined themselves in terms of their opposition to the world.[40]

The implications of Schneiders' analysis for the diocesan priesthood should be clear. While not called to live in monasteries or in vowed apostolic communities, diocesan priests were to be "in the world but not of it." The new *rapprochement* with the world, therefore, effected a similar Copernican revolution for the diocesan priest and those contemplating a vocation to the diocesan priesthood.

Cultural Considerations

Earlier in this chapter we considered the implications of the relatively low birth rate (about 1.85 children) of U.S. Catholic households on the vocation issue. Linked to this demographic reality is the increased number of single-parent Catholic families. Approximately half of the young men and women making vocational or career decisions are doing so in an environment that has been marked by separation, divorce, or death. Parental encouragement may still be there as well as an atmosphere of family prayer, but in today's church only one third of Catholic families currently celebrate Mass each weekend. A generation ago, approximately 70 percent of Catholics attended church each week. What can we make of the apparent correlation between the drop in vocations and the drop in Mass attendance?[41]

A new Enlightenment? The church's long-standing battle with the new order spawned by the Enlightenment came to a head, as we saw in chapter two, with Pope Pius X's 1907 encyclical *Pascendi dominici gregis* condemning the heresy of Modernism. The Enlightenment's child, modernity, brought forth in turn extraordinary breakthroughs in science, the arts, commerce, and industry. Modernity also had a shadow side which was rightly challenged by the church—secularism, scientism, radical empiricism, rationalism, and the dismissal of any dimension of transcendent reality, to name but a few of its forms. Shadow side not-withstanding, modernity's revolutionary contributions to humankind were staggering and its many positive forms were finally recognized by the church at Vatican II. But just as the church finally came to terms with modernity, the curtain was being raised on yet another major historical force still taking form on humanity's literary and philosophical stage. Cultural critics speak of it as "postmodernity." If the curtain continues to rise, the church will be faced with challenges to its mission and message that may well be unprecedented. Certainly, it will match the challenge the church found in responding to the Enlightenment. Consider the title of Walter Truett Anderson's book on the postmodern world: *Reality Isn't What It Used To Be.* It really comes down to that. Postmodernism, still coming into focus, promises in its present inchoate form to reshape our understanding of reality. Anderson writes:

> [It] is a story about stories, a belief about beliefs, and in time—probably a very short time—it will become a central part of the worldview of most people. It will be the core of the first global civilization. But it is not yet a core. It is more a seed of discontent. It fills our daily lives with uncertainty and anxiety, renders us vulnerable to tyrants and cults, shakes religious faith, and divides societies into groups contending with one another in a strange and unfamiliar kind of ideological conflict: not merely conflict *between* beliefs, but conflict *about* belief itself.[42]

A decade later, cultural historian and cultural critic Morris Berman writes of the postmodern world:

> By 1989, what had been an arcane French academic discussion about the world as text and the absence of meaning reached popular consciousness. In dozens of ways, the nihilism of deconstruction played

itself out in a new kind of everyday sensibility: The president had become . . . a kind of corporate CEO, with no moral or personal responsibilities; the individual not only had no identity, he didn't *need* an identity, and could reinvent himself continuously; choices were only a matter of what worked, and therefore had no existential or ethical meaning (and hence, were essentially equivalent); and finally . . . no values were superior to any other values, because there was no such thing as the truth, and therefore all realities were interchangeable, so the major activity became mindless consumption.[43]

Robert Schreiter reminds us that not only do modernism and postmodernism overlap, but in many parts of the world, the premodern continues to interact with modern and postmodern influences. The emerging postmodern complex of mindsets, therefore, does not negate the modern nor even, in some areas of the globe, the premodern. Postmodernity, Schreiter writes, "is a combine of different options. . . . It assumes the modern, but tries to move behind it, ahead with it or beyond it in selected ways. The coexistence of the premodern, the modern and the postmodern constitutes a hermeneutic lens through which to view the immediate future."[44]

Postmodernism, in its various manifestations, means to rattle if not shake the very foundations of long-held worldviews and belief systems. I raise the subject here because it remains at this point in our history one of the major challenges—if not *the* major challenge—to vocations to the priesthood and religious life. It announces not only the loss of a unifying worldview that previously gave meaning and purpose to the sacrifices inherent to priesthood and religious life, but it challenges the validity of belief systems themselves. If the Enlightenment led to scientism and secularism, postmodernism provokes a radical relativism and the collapse of the transcendent. The unconscious, collectively shared vision of "Catholic" reality and its sustaining myths that formed the Catholic imagination—thereby providing immense religious capital to a life of service as a priest or religious—is now being undercut by a literary-philosophical force that for most people remains shrouded in mysterious jargon. Nonetheless, its undercurrents, in my judgment, are influencing the career and vocational decisions of our young men and women.[45]

Postmodern thinkers and theorists, therefore, deserve our attention. Without a readiness to understand this perplexing cultural phenomenon, our fears and anxieties will only become more paralyzing. What they are proposing may indeed require decades before it eclipses the declining, yet controlling, modernism of our day. And its influence is likely to be short-lived in the overall scheme of things. Yet it cannot be willed away. In the present cultural milieu, it seems naïve at best to be praying for religious vocations without first, or at least at the same time, praying for the wisdom to "read the signs of our times" in order to pass on to future generations the saving message of the gospel in a world that now suspects there is no saving message, no saving truth.

In this period of profound cultural transition, the vocational "truth" of some Christians will be to serve as light in the midst of the descending darkness and prophetic voice in the midst of disintegrating structures. Such women and men will possess souls motivated by a passion for what matters most, and they will be women and men on a mission. The very meaningfulness of their lives will be a blessing to the community and their sense of mission will give direction and hope to their sisters and brothers. However, they will only be drawn to service in a church that faces even hard truths about itself with honesty and integrity. Ecclesial cultures of denial and evasion, of secrecy and status, will not appeal to them.

Unfortunately, signs of denial and evasion are all about us. And with notable exceptions, the emerging cultural ethos and its impact on the life and mission of the church in general and religious vocations in particular is commonly ignored by church leaders and vocation directors.[46] The more is the pity.

CHAPTER SIX

ABUSE OF OUR CHILDREN

Let's get the question straight. What explains the tragic worldwide explosion of sexual abuse by priests and other religious personnel? These men and women were presumably trained over many years in seminaries and religious houses to understand and practice chastity as a condition of their calling. How could they, then, suddenly have found unresolved sexual problems bringing intractable pain to those thy abused and incomparable suffering to themselves?

—Eugene Kennedy

As I BEGIN THIS REFLECTION on the church's response to the sexual abuse of minors by clergy and religious, the case of sixty-six-year-old Boston priest John J. Geoghan is making headlines and garnering time on national television news programs. The latest in a line of priest abusers brought to public attention, Geoghan stands convicted of abusing a ten-year-old boy and faces further criminal prosecution as well as scores of civil suits relating to his alleged abuse of at least 130 victims.[1] Unsealed church records and legal documents, according to media reports, reveal that church authorities knew of the priest's propensity to abuse young boys for more than fifteen years. The documents, we are told, show little concern for his victims and a puzzling gentleness from Geoghan's ecclesiastical superiors.

The Boston scandal is a clear signal that the ordeal rocking the church for the last twenty years is, sadly, alive and virulent. In the final years of the 1990s, hopes were expressed in church circles that the tragic scandals involving the sexual abuse of children by

priests, bishops, and religious were waning. Perhaps, it was
thought, it would finally go away. Such hopes were dashed. The
wound, it now appears, was never properly diagnosed, never properly treated.[2] Furthermore, church officials seemed to learn little
from the tragic errors made in the 1980s and 1990s while responding to the victims' reports of abuse and from decisions to re-
assign clergy predators. Clearly, progress was made in the
protocols for responding to allegations of clergy and religious sexual abuse. For example, bishops and diocesan officials have generally responded more pastorally, with greater sensitivity and
compassion for the victims and their families, than they did in the
1980s and early 1990s.[3]

We should take, I think, little comfort in this attempt of the
church to respond more pastorally, less "corporately," to cases of
clergy sexual abuse of minors because important questions, as we
shall see shortly, have been avoided and when raised have been
greeted with silence. What, for example, is the meaning of these
wide-ranging incidents of clergy sexual abuse of minors? I suspect
it is more than a matter of the flesh being weak. Could there be
structural or systemic factors at play here? These questions simply were never posed. Instead church authorities proposed that
the problem was, indeed, human weakness involving a few bad apples. Some put the blame on a breakdown in church discipline and
faulty education and formation in our seminaries. Still others
pointed to a morally bankrupt culture spilling over into the ranks
of pastors and other church leaders. It's likely these factors have
some relevance here. But the silence holds. There is no sustained,
honest effort being made to address the issue head on, to get to
the bottom of one of the greatest scandals ever to rock the church.
Before we examine the pastoral and structural implications of the
scandal, some attention should be paid to still other forms of denial that have surfaced in the years following the first scandals in
the early 1980s.

Faces of Denial

I draw here on the important work of A. Richard Sipe who has identified the different faces of denial that are commonly presented when the problem of clergy abuse of children and teens is raised.[4] Sipe is a longtime observer of and commentator on the priesthood whose research and writing wrestles with the meaning beneath the numbers and statistics of clergy sexual misconduct. Consider the rationalizations Sipe identifies:

There is no problem; it can't be true. No longer heard today, this bold assertion was common only a decade ago. It was broken down by admissions of abuse by priests and bishops and the preponderance of evidence which led to widely publicized civil and criminal trials. It calls to mind the alleged comment of a cardinal who boasted, "I only lie in the best interests of the church."

Abuse by priests may exist, but it is very rare. We know now that tens of thousands of cases of clergy sexual abuse have been recorded and verified.[5] The number of priest abusers in the U.S. alone is estimated to be in the thousands. Yet the Vatican frames the scandal differently. In a January 10, 2002, interview with Vatican Radio, Archbishop Tarcisio Bertone, secretary of the Congregation for the Doctrine of Faith, expressed regret that the priesthood as a whole has been "offended" by the behavior of "a few persons, a few ministers, when almost the totality of ministers behaves in an exemplary manner."[6] A different perspective on the scandal was taken by a bishop who told me that there is not a single diocese in the United States that has gone unscathed.

The media distorts everything. Sipe notes that, "Cardinal Law of Boston voiced a notable public attack against the press when he called down the wrath of God on *The Boston Globe* for printing stories [in 1992] about Fr. James Porter and his victims in Massachusetts."[7] The Geoghan case mentioned above certainly undermines the cardinal's protest. His criticism of the media, however, was shared by large numbers of Catholics and people sympathetic to the church, especially when the misconduct scandals began appearing in the early 1980s.

Clifford Longley, writing in the international Catholic weekly *The Tablet*, commented on the role of the media in the resignation of a British archbishop in the fall of 2001: "It is being claimed that Archbishop Ward of Cardiff was forced to resign 'after a media campaign against him.' This phrase implies that the media's role was somehow mischievous, disloyal and illegitimate."[8] What especially irked Longley was the suggestion that the Cardiff affair was none of the press's business. Incredibly, the notion still holds in some quarters that a whole range of church issues, from fiscal malfeasance to child abuse is "none of the press's business." The church makes a serious mistake, I believe, when it perceives the media as intractably its enemy. Wagons are circled, legitimate questions from reporters are deflected, and questionable strategies employed to hide documentation from both the media and attorneys representing victims and their families. In many cases the media rightly suspects a cover-up. In this climate largely created by the church itself, it is naïve to think the press would not pursue these stories with focused tenacity.

The problem is no worse than in other religious groups or in the general population. Perhaps this assertion isn't a rationalization or a form of denial at all. Certainly the scandal of sexual abuse has surfaced in clergy of other faiths and denominations. Most pedophiles, it is commonly noted, are married men; though not surprising in light of the fact that there is a much larger population of married men than celibate Catholic priests. The scandal, then, clearly isn't restricted to Catholic clergy nor is there an inherent relationship, in itself, between Catholic clergy abuse and celibacy. Still, the evidence suggests there is a higher incidence of abuse among Catholic clergy than the population at large. Sipe insists it would not be that difficult to discover the actual extent of abuse among priests and other church personnel. The church could simply poll bishops and religious superiors asking them for the numbers of credible allegations brought against their priests and religious. These figures could then be compared to existing research measuring the incidence of sexual abuse of minors in the population at large.[9] They could also serve to verify or contest the current estimate that 7 to 10 percent of priests are caught in the web of clergy abuse. Whatever the numbers and however they compare to the findings of researchers, the cases already part of the public record suggest they would be sufficiently large to merit probing inquiries into the *meaning* of sexual abuse by clergy. Only after the church comes to a better understanding of the etiology and nature of these tragic behaviors as they relate to clergy can it address them appropriately. Both the welfare of our young and the future viability and credibility of our priests and bishops are at stake here.

They wanted it—they liked it. Sipe cites a Canadian bishop who claimed that clergy abuse was the result of "streetwise youngsters seducing naïve clergy."[10] Most, if not all, of the world's major cities find themselves dealing with prostitution in one form or another, even prostitution involving children and teenagers. There are, tragically, teenage boys (and girls) forced into offering sex in return for money and goods. We know, too, that teenagers can be seductive.[11] Furthermore, false allegations have indeed been brought against innocent priests—and a notable cardinal—by teenagers and young men. The damage and pain they have inflicted should not be minimized or overlooked. But the majority of allegations of misconduct by priests, religious, and bishops against minors that come to light seem to have merit. It is disingenuous to suggest that the problem can be traced to streetwise youngsters seducing naïve clergy. Even in cases where a minor has in fact seduced a member of the clergy, the "victim" who blames the minor for seducing him denies his own moral responsibility as an adult, a responsibility enhanced by his role as a public, religious leader. Still attempts continue to be made to blame the victims. As incredible as it sounds, a chancery official of the Diocese of Dallas, commenting after a jury found the diocese liable for abuses by Dallas priest Rudy Kos, proposed that the victims themselves had to assume some responsibility for the abuse. The victims "knew what was right and what was wrong. Anybody who reaches the age of reason shares responsibility for what they do."[12] He went on to suggest that the parents of the victims shared some of the blame for not being more alert to the possibility of such harm coming to their sons. Whenever this form of denial surfaces, victims are victimized again. And it is rightly perceived to be a scandal itself.

Other manifestations of denial listed by Sipe include: *abusers are sick; the consequences are not dire and the victim was sick anyway; Father is only human; forgive and forget; we are not responsible for abuse—it is just a few bad apples.*[13] Some of these protestations, no matter how much the evidence discredits them, continue to be heard. How can this be?

One Abuser's Rationalization

The British writer John Cornwell provides a rare glimpse into the mind of a priest abuser. The rationalization seems untroubled, without concern for the welfare of the intended victim, and frightening in its earnestness. It may be far from typical, but still remains, I believe, instructive. Cornwell writes:

> Not long before he died, one of my close priest friends who had a position of responsibility as chaplain in a Catholic residential college told me on his sixty-ninth birthday that he was currently attempting to seduce an eighteen-year-old male student into a sexual liaison. Wise and evidently good in countless ways, he was a stirring preacher and a man who loved his priesthood, but I came to see that his life was profoundly dislocated. I realized that although I had been acquainted with him for twenty-five years, I hardly knew him at all. He said, "I'm convinced that I cannot become fully human until I've had sexual relations with this young man." At one point he said, "Oh, the body is just a playground; it's the soul that matters."[14]

Cornwell, concerned about the welfare of the young man, tried to dissuade his priest friend. How his friend responded to Cornwell's urgings, we don't know. The priest, we are told, died suddenly soon afterward. His story is both sad and chilling. We can only wonder

if it reflects the perspective of other priest abusers. There appears
to be no wrestling with the demands of the gospel, with the violation of boundaries, with the harm the young man would suffer.
I suspect clergy education programs on boundary issues and the
tragic effects of sexual abuse on minors would have had little impact on this priest. From our brief glimpse into his thinking and desiring, Cornwell's priest friend appears remarkably at ease, even at
peace. I think he would have nodded a silent yes to Ellis Hanson's
opening paragraphs to his chapter "Priests and Acolytes" in his
Decadence and Catholicism:

> I have often been asked in the course of writing this book why a
> gay man or a lover of boys would become a priest. The motives are
> so numerous, however, that the real question ought to be why
> straight men become priests. Beyond faith, which I gather to be the
> primary appeal, since the priesthood would be unbearable without
> it, there are other motivations for men of a certain inclination: the
> effeminized pastoral persona, the pleasures of ritual, public trust
> and respect, freedom from the social pressure to marry, opportuni-
> ties for intimacy with boys, passionate friendship and cohabitation
> with likeminded men and a discipline for coping with sexual shame
> and guilt.
>
> I can think of no better argument for the homoeroticism of
> the priesthood than the pederastic priest-and-acolyte narratives
> that proliferated in England between 1880 and about 1930. I say
> pederastic because there is a significant trace of the Greek in their
> idealized cult of devotion between man and boy, but it is a cult that
> the Church has promoted, despite its formal disavowals, by ren-
> dering the priesthood one of the most attractive occupations avail-
> able to men who love boys.[15]

Church authorities have yet to study carefully the rationalizations
of priest abusers and their understanding of chastity and celibacy.
The results of such studies, I'm convinced, would be disturbing,
perhaps profoundly disturbing, yet essential to any long-term
resolution to the present scandals.[16]

In the meantime, consider the implications that may be drawn from the chaplain's wish to seduce the young man. While the eighteen-year-old was legally an adult, he was just months away from being under age. The priest's desire to seduce him into a sexual liaison remains a serious moral, if not legal, abuse of power and station. We might wonder how many other young men fell under the covetous eye of Cornwell's friend? How many may have been approached? How many have been seduced? Did his sexual interest in young men come to the attention of the college's administration or faculty? If so, was he confronted? Was his sexual interest picked up by the students? It is likely that at least some of the students knew of his predilection for handsome young men. How did that knowledge affect their regard and respect for the priesthood? And then, what can be made of his most provocative confession: "I'm convinced that I cannot become fully human until I've had sexual relations with this young man"? He suggests with these words a moral imperative to have sexual relations with the young man in question. This from a "stirring preacher and a man who loved his priesthood."

One gets the impression that the senior priest is pleased with his assignment to the college and pleased with his life as a priest. Furthermore, his almost casual admission to Cornwell implies he is neither embarrassed by his seductive wish nor troubled by it. Can it be that other priests who violate sacred boundaries with parishioners or youngsters also feel a moral imperative to do so in order to become fully human? It may be impossible to pursue that question, but whether or not it is rare or common in priests and bishops who act out sexually, it may be an important clue to understanding the mindset of clergy who abuse minors and others.

What's at Stake

Quite simply, quite a bit is at stake here. The implications of clergy abuse of children are, I propose, far-reaching and tightly-interrelated, creating the possibility of a domino effect which, with one slight nudge, could bring about structural changes and pastoral challenges that may well affect the church at large. From the perspective of what's at stake, the denial, though not excusable, is understandable—especially for believers who hold to a static, ahistorical vision of the church. The implications, as I read them, fall into three clusters—pastoral, fiscal, and systemic.

Pastoral Implications

Thousands upon thousands of young victims have suffered the almost unimaginable effects of sexual abuse at the hands of Catholic clergy. I've sat with some of them and listened to their halting attempts to put into words the pain, confusion, disillusionment, and sense of shame that followed the episodes of abuse. Some feel confused about their sexual orientation, unable to forget that their sexual initiation occurred with an older member of the same sex. Most, I suspect, carry wounds that will be healed only over time, if at all. Based on the stories of the relatively few victims I have met, many, I believe, are angry at the betrayal they suffered. Many others hold no hatred in their hearts; only the passionate wish that no other young people be hurt.[17]

Their parents' pain can only be imagined. Should they have been suspicious of the priest or priests who befriended their son or daughter? And in some cases, their sons and daughters? Often their pain and the pain of their children is intensified by the suspicion and defensive posturing of church officials to whom they report the abuse. The hurt, of course, goes beyond the victim and his or her family. It spreads to siblings, cousins, grandparents, aunts and uncles, friends and neighbors. Reports indicate there are approximately 100,000 victims of clergy misconduct in the U.S. alone. The harm inflicted on their family members and friends is likely to raise the number directly touched by the scandal to a million. When the dismay and hurt of the accused priest's parishioners are factored in, the number affected could be in the millions. The devastating effect on the credibility and trustworthiness of Catholic clergy is incalculable.

Not only in families and communities coping with first-hand experiences of clergy sex abuse, but throughout the Catholic population in general, the high esteem and respect traditionally accorded to bishops, priests, and religious have waned considerably. Some of the victims and their families say it is gone forever. Priests themselves sense a dampening of the trust and confidence parishioners have traditionally placed in them. *Boston Globe* religion reporter Michael Paulson, in a story addressing the impact of the Geoghan scandal on priests, writes:

> The crisis of clergy sexual abuse has taken an enormous toll on the Catholic Church, harming victims and their families and shattering the faith of many others. But the crisis has also been devastating for the vast majority of priests who are not child molesters. Accused of nothing, they find their own lives dramatically transformed by the abusive behavior of others, and by the occasional failure of the church they love to detect, deter, or to stop that abuse.[18]

Priests know they shouldn't take it personally but the derisive caricatures now commonplace in cartoons, jokes, and comedy acts— and in overheard conversations, hurt nonetheless. Fr. Bob Bowers, a Boston priest interviewed by *The Boston Globe* in the story cited above, tells of a friend who returned from a Halloween party "shocked that someone showed up dressed as a pedophile priest."[19] With their integrity and credibility under suspicion, their preaching, counseling, indeed the entire range of their pastoral care becomes more challenging, more arduous. The long-term effects on their emotional and spiritual lives remain to be seen.

Obviously pained by the harm done to countless victims of clergy abuse in almost every part of the world and aware of the discouragement it has evoked in his priests, John Paul II issued a moving apology in *Ecclesia in Oceania*, the concluding document to the 1998 Synod for Oceania, which he released via the internet on November 22, 2001:

> Sexual abuse by some clergy and religious has caused great suffering and spiritual harm to the victims. It has been very damaging in

the life of the church. . . . Sexual abuse within the church is a profound contradiction of the teaching and witness of Jesus Christ.

Those participating in the synod, the Pope said, wish to "apologize unreservedly to the victims for the pain and disillusionment caused to them." They also want "open and just procedures to respond to complaints in this area" and want to offer "compassionate and effective care for the victims, their families, and the whole community and the offenders themselves."[20]

The disillusionment mentioned by the Pope certainly cannot help the already serious vocation picture. Priests still play significant roles in the lives of their parishioners. The laity in the postconciliar church, generally well-educated and fair-minded, readily distinguish the priest abusers from the committed and faithful priests ministering in their midst. But these same parishioners have no illusions about the difficulties and dangers inherent in the contemporary priesthood. To what extent Catholic parents might encourage a son interested in the priesthood remains uncertain. In the climate of the last decades of the church's history, we should not be surprised if Catholic parents would actively dissuade a son from considering the priesthood as his vocation.

Fiscal Implications

It is estimated that in the U.S. alone more than one billion dollars has been paid out of diocesan coffers and religious order treasuries to victims of sexual abuse by clergy. Insurance companies bore some of the financial burden in the early years of the scandal, but they offer no protection to the church at the beginning of the twenty-first century. And the financial implications of the numerous civil suits in the Geoghan case and other cases now pending no doubt will require an upward adjustment of the one-billion-dollar estimate. It is difficult to imagine U.S. dioceses (and parishes) not being significantly threatened, even drastically affected, by these enormous drains on their resources. Some have already had to deal with catastrophic losses bringing them to the brink of bankruptcy.

Still, the fiscal condition of the U.S. church remains unclear. Joseph Claude Harris, in a 1997 *America* essay, paints a positive picture of the overall fiscal strength of Catholic dioceses and parishes while acknowledging differing assessments. Drawing on Harris' research, *The Boston Globe* reported that currently $8.2 billion a year is collected at the parish level:[21]

> Confusion clouds current discussions of U.S. Catholic Church finances. Available facts conflict with pronouncements from leadership groups. Net funds contributed to parishes grew by $1.1 billion between 1990 and 1994. Schools generated an additional $1.3 billion over the same time span. Yet the Catholic Common Ground Project listed "dwindling financial support from parishioners" as a serious problem confronting parish managers. . . . Additional billions and anxiety over impending bankruptcy do not seem to belong together in the same conversation.[22]

Near broke or solvent, the horizon harbors gathering storm clouds for each and every diocese in the U.S. Whatever the church's fiscal strength might be—and it is important to remember that it varies greatly from diocese to diocese—the clergy abuse scandal is proving to be a serious, even grave, threat to the church's financial resources. And churches elsewhere as well.

An Associated Press story out of Dublin in January 2002 reported:

> After years of denial and painful negotiations, the Roman Catholic Church in Ireland agreed . . . to pay $110 million to Irish children who were sexually abused by priests, nuns and other church officials in decades past. The landmark deal was designed to conclude a 10-year struggle by the church in this predominantly Catholic nation to overcome sex scandals involving its clergy going back to the 1940s.[23]

The breadth and depth of the international scandal—and that's what it is—remains difficult to gauge in the present climate of secrecy, a climate reinforced by a Vatican directive, sent in Latin to bishops and religious superiors in May 2001 (but only published by the Vatican in December) requiring major superiors of religious orders to forward cases of clergy misconduct with minors to the Congregation of the Doctrine of Faith for judication.[24] There, the cases will be processed in secret, it is explained, to protect the rights of victims, the church, and the accused priests.

Whatever the real scope of the scandal might be, should the total monetary amount awarded by courts to victims of clergy abuse in North America and Europe ever be tabulated, the sum would be staggering. Add to that total the amounts paid by the church for the counseling of victims, for the treatment of clergy abusers (it's not unusual for a diocese or a religious order to spend over $100,000 for in-patient treatment of a single priest abuser), and for countless out-of-court settlements that have avoided public disclosure, and the figures would be significantly higher.

Monies paid out to some victims have been and continue to be substantial, but no matter the amount, money alone cannot heal or compensate for the spiritual and emotional harm inflicted on thousands of youngsters by Catholic clergy and religious. That, of course, is the real tragedy here.

As the church slowly turns to face the full implications of the abuse tragedy, it continues steadfastly, even heroically, to meet the basic needs of men, women, and children throughout the world who are struggling desperately to simply survive. Catholic missionaries—priests, religious, and lay—can be found in the poorest of countries working to awaken a true sense of human dignity in the hearts of the world's poor and starving. They mirror the efforts of priests, religious, and lay ministers serving in the poorest neighborhoods of our cities, with anxious immigrants and underpaid migrant workers. These missionaries and pastoral ministers deserve generous financial support. So do Catholic social service agencies, social action programs, and Catholic schools. Sooner or later, if it is not the case already, the clergy abuse scandals threaten that support.

The fact remains that the financial factor, while of secondary consequence in light of the personal harm inflicted on the victims of clergy abuse, threatens to undercut the pastoral mission of the church.

Structural Implications

There is mounting concern both within the walls of the Vatican and beyond that the ongoing scandals of clergy sexual abuse are weakening the church's already strained rationale supporting mandatory celibacy for Latin rite priests (Eastern rite Catholic priests in Europe are not bound to celibacy).[25] With the significant drop in students preparing for the priesthood and the graying of the clergy, mandatory celibacy continues to be questioned by the laity, by rank and file priests, and by some members of the hierarchy. When we add to this mounting ferment the obvious psychosexual immaturity linked with the abuse of teenagers and, in the cases of pedophilia, the tenacious psychopathologies associated with the abuse of prepubescent children, the questioning of mandatory celibacy for Latin rite priests, at least in progressive circles of the church, becomes all the more incessant.

At no time since the clergy abuse scandal broke two decades ago has the official church acknowledged a significant dimension to the entire sad affair. The silence, I believe, is calculated. When priests and bishops have abused teenagers, the vast majority of the victims have been boys. There have indeed been cases of clergy abuse of teenage girls, but a clear majority of the victims have been boys.[26] Acknowledging this important factor, some fear, would call attention to the growing realization that large numbers of Catholic clergy are gay. And, furthermore, it might be concluded, rightly or wrongly, that a significant number of the gay clergy appear to be psychosexually immature. Immature adults, we know, find healthy friendships with their own age group difficult. Relationships with minors, on the other hand, or with young seminarians as is sometimes the case, are less threatening. Let me make explicit what I assume to be obvious: Emotionally mature priests and bishops, whether straight or gay, do not engage in sexual contact with minors. Nor do they find their primary emotional fulfillment in significant relationships with minors or individuals considerably younger than themselves.

From the perspective outlined here, the clergy abuse scandal may be read as yet another indicator that mandatory celibacy isn't working. Indeed, the suspicion grows that it may foster or reinforce, at least in some, the very psychosexual immaturity that leads to compulsive and diverse manifestations of destructive behavior. What's at stake here, then, is the very structural undergirding of mandatory celibacy for Latin rite priests. In this light, the silence is hardly surprising.

Celibacy, moreover, is a cornerstone of the infrastructure of the Catholic ecclesiastical world. Tamper with its foundational role in the Latin rite, *the* rite of the church, and the consequences will likely prove far-reaching. Lines of authority, appointments to the episcopacy, parish life as we know it now, the role of women in church leadership, would all be significantly affected. If celibacy is indeed at the core of the present ecclesial order, those unreservedly committed to mandated celibacy for diocesan priests will be inclined—perhaps on an unconscious level—to remain silent about realities and patterns of behavior that connect sexual abuse, emotional immaturity, and sexual orientation with mandatory celibacy. How long they will be able to remain silent is another question.

Asking the Right Questions

No one expects church officials to assume the role of psychoanalyst with "crozier and miter" probing the psyches of abusers to find deeply imbedded psychological and emotional pathologies. That is not the role of church leadership. But it is the role of church leaders to determine if church systems and structures, no matter how unintended, no matter how indirectly, might be contributing to the present sad phenomenon shaking its foundations.

Evil—cold, calculating, seductive—confounds the human spirit. From a faith perspective, a perspective that holds the human heart and will are embraced by the very spirit and mercy of God, it is inexplicable. Destructive, violating actions against our young by the church's own ministers of the gospel are particularly incomprehensible. Nevertheless, church authorities must do more than pastorally respond to the cases that come to their attention. There is an urgent need to ask questions that might seem, from an institutional perspective, unthinkable.

Before even a tentative effort to formulate the right questions relating to the clergy abuse scandal, the powerful emotional charge associated with the violation of children and teens needs to be acknowledged. For the same emotional current is likely to surface both in serious discussions and even in casual conversations about such a topic. I argue here that an effort needs to be made to suspend, at least for the time being, moral judgment which only intensifies the emotional charge inherent to the discussion. Failure to do so narrowly focuses attempts to get at the why or meaning of the scandal to the personal culpability of the offender. Efforts to understand the meaning of the abuse, the *why* of it, then, become exercises in analysis, as we have seen, a kind of psychoanalytic probing into the arrested erotic desires of the offender, his complex of rationalizations, and, of course, his moral culpability. While these issues have their place, especially for the therapeutic treatment of abusers, the question of meaning as I propose it here is more contextual. Could it be that institutional forms of church life and formation, long held to be sacred and effective, are no longer sacred and effective?

Certainly the abuse of children is a terrible thing. And when the abuse comes from priests, bishops, and religious it is all the more appalling. Without minimizing the harm done, can we avoid demonizing the offender? For the offender may be a victim himself—not of the minors he has abused—but of a complex of forces, personal and structural, which he himself may not understand.

An honest effort to get at the meaning behind the scandal might begin with the following factors that define clergy sexual abuse, factors which have, for the most part, gone unacknowledged by institutional leaders:

- As noted above, victims of clergy sexual abuse are predominantly, but not exclusively, teenaged boys. While there are pedophiles in the ranks of the clergy—James Porter of the Fall River Diocese who was convicted in 1992 and John Geoghan of the Archdiocese of Boston who was convicted in 2002 immediately come to mind—true pedophiles are sexually attracted to prepubescent children.[27] The distinction, subtle to some, remains important from a clinical and therapeutic perspective. Apparently the targeting of young boys by clerical predators is proving particularly disturbing to church authorities for they never speak of it. Fairly or unfairly, it points to the disproportionate number of gay priests and seminarians that in turn raises the mandatory celibacy issue mentioned above. And the celibacy issue cannot be raised by bishops and other officials without risking the displeasure of the Vatican.

- Many of the clergy abusers show little genuine remorse and few signs of genuine concern for their victims.[28] While there are exceptions to this observation concerning the absence of remorse held by a number of diocesan vicars of clergy with whom I have spoken, it suggests that the abuser himself is emotionally wounded and, in many cases, was abused himself as a youth.

- The abuse of some victims went on for years. It's likely, in light of this reality, that many abusers who established long-term relationships weren't really struggling to bring a halt to the abuse. How did conscience formation take place in these men? Or better, how explain the absence of conscience formation in

men who spent years in seminary formation? "I came
to regard [clergy abusers] as focused sociopaths—little
or no moral sense, no feelings of guilt and remorse for
what they had done at least in this area of their lives.
. . ."[29] Andrew Sullivan tells of a victim who reported, "After he molested me, he would bless me. . . .
It's very confusing. . . . After we did these things,
he'd put his hand on my head and make the sign of
the cross."[30]

- The number of clergy abuse victims is far greater than
the number of cases that have come to the attention of
both church and civil authorities. The average number
of victims of a single abuser is estimated to be in the
hundreds.[31] Andrew Greeley, as early as 1993, estimated that 100,000 men and women had been abused
by 2,500 priests—6 percent of priests in the United
States."[32] Still, as we have seen, some church officials
continue to define the scandal as a "few bad apples"
each abusing one or two youngsters.

Each of these factors, to a greater or lesser degree, has been
denied or deflected by church leaders since the scandal broke in
the early 1980s. Addressing the culture of secrecy that shaped the
church's response to the clergy abuse scandals, *Time Magazine*'s
Johanna McGeary writes:

Dioceses lapsed into a pattern of denial and deception. They treated
sexual pathology as a moral failure and crime as a religious matter.
The Roman Catholic Church is a stern hierarchy that has always
kept its deliberations secret, policed itself and issued orders from
the top. An obedient priest moves up in power by keeping his head
down, winning rewards for bureaucratic skills and strict orthodoxy.
When Cardinals are created, they take a vow before the Pope to
"keep in confidence anything that, if revealed, would cause a scandal or harm to the church." When it came to sex abuse, the Vatican

essentially told bishops, You're on your own. But if saving the church from scandal was literally a cardinal virtue, then the bishops of America's 194 dioceses who had direct responsibility for priestly misconduct would make it their first principle. Better by far never to let the public know.[33]

Only after the abuse began making headlines—and after strong criticism of the media for reporting the scandal—did the voices of denial soften. Finally, significant positive steps were taken, not to get to the meaning behind the abusive behaviors but to respond more pastorally and effectively to reports of clergy misconduct.[34] Diocesan initiated action to this date includes the publication of diocesan policies to be followed when allegations of misconduct are brought against priests and other church personnel; special review committees to determine if a priest, after treatment, is suitable for reassignment; and clergy education programs dealing with human sexuality and boundary issues. Each of these initiatives is evidence of church efforts to assist the victims, to protect children from abuse, to protect diocesan resources, and to avoid further scandal. However, church leaders continue to frame the scandal as primarily a problem of human weakness and failed personal responsibility. Even the recent Vatican decision requiring religious superiors to forward cases of clergy misconduct to the Congregation for the Doctrine of Faith to ensure canonical due process, insists that such reporting and deliberations be secret.

Sexual Teaching

In the Catholic world, any deliberate, free expression of human sexuality, whether in thought, word, or deed, outside of heterosexual marriage (and always open to the possibility of procreation), is judged to be immoral and therefore sinful. And not only sinful, but seriously sinful; one's very salvation is always at stake. Furthermore, open discussion in seminaries and houses of formation about human sexuality, sexual orientation, and sexual

longing is guarded, even discouraged, except in the most confidential of contexts—spiritual direction and the rite of reconciliation.

Douglas Dandurand, researching the implications of mandated celibacy on the spiritual and emotional development of
Catholic clergy, reports a gay priest's reflection of his coming to
terms with his orientation during his seminary years and the advice he received from his spiritual director: "It was . . . made very
clear to me by the spiritual director and counselor that I visited
with . . . [telling me to] 'make sure that you don't tell the rector.
Make sure you don't tell the vice-rector. You've got to be very careful who knows about this.' . . . And you knew some staff would
use it against you."[35]

Because in the Catholic moral system, sin is closely linked to
human sexuality, it is feared that open discussion of sexuality
might lead to what has been traditionally understood as "a manifestation of conscience"—concern that one might publicly reveal
the state of one's soul in such discussions. The taboo associated
with honest, open discussions of sexuality, of course, goes beyond
our seminaries and houses of formation and can be found in many
quarters of the church and even in some quarters of society. In such
a climate, future celibates know what is expected of them even in
the years of their seminary formation: a life devoid of sexual expression and even of sexual fantasy. If their efforts to meet those
expectations are not supported by honest, informed dialogue and
are not modeled by healthy, integrated professors, the years ahead
are fraught with danger. And the seminary system itself is un-
veiled as part of the problem.

A system, in this case an ecclesial system, suspicious of the
fundamental value and goodness of human sexuality demands exceptional emotional and psychosexual maturity of its candidates
for the priesthood. Without such unusual qualities of personality
and character, seminarians are likely to make attempts to ignore
their sexual energies and interests; in other words, repress them.
Eventually, repression rebels. Renouncing a sexual life and at the
same time often preoccupied with sex, a seminarian is likely to be

disposed during his seminary years or well into his priesthood to unhealthy and even profoundly destructive expressions of sexuality. Consider Eberhard Schaetzing's definition of ecclesiogenic neurosis: "[T]he syndrome is caused by the widespread tabooizing education in which the sexual and erotic areas of life are banned from open discussion and are considered to be immoral, forbidden or even threatened with punishment."[36] And so we return to the question: Is it possible that our present ecclesial system—as well as the ecclesial systems of other religious denominations—is a factor in the etiology of the sexual abuse of minors by clergy and religious?

The question, it should be noted, has already been asked, directly or indirectly, by a number of writers and researchers—most recently by Eugene Kennedy in his insightful book *The Unhealed Wound*. And the question is raised in the private discussions of Catholic parents and seminary personnel, but it hasn't been asked by church authorities, except, perhaps, behind closed doors. I believe the institutional church's silence is understandable, but, again, indefensible. The question and the answers it elicits would no doubt spotlight long-standing ecclesial structures that, over time, have been identified with that which is essential to the church. While the structures are historically conditioned, they are embraced in some quarters as central to the church's identity and mission. Does our present seminary system, for example, provide the best environment and training for our future priests? Is mandatory celibacy for Latin rite priests still optimal in today's church? Questions like these would no doubt call attention to the church's overall teaching on human sexuality and increase the already serious tensions and disagreements in this sensitive area. Resistance to such questions and the evaluations they imply, however, is inhibiting a critically important dialogue that needs to be joined, in my opinion, as soon as possible.

In the meantime, we might prepare for this hoped-for dialogue by carefully considering Kennedy's thesis. As long as we pit nature against spirit, he argues, we remain a wounded people, a wounded church. Church leaders who fail to understand our common woundedness, look upon nature as something to be subdued, even conquered. Instead of joyfully trusting in the goodness of creation, in God's abiding presence, (without denying, of course, the reality of sin) we wounded deny even our wounds, often compensating for our unnamed pain through willful exercises of power and subjugation. Our exercise of authority, in particular, becomes distorted and twisted if our wound is allowed to go untended.

Before leaving this sad and painful reflection on Catholic clergy's sexual abuse of minors and the denial and minimization that has sorely exacerbated the scandal, a final note related to the Geoghan case is in order.[37] When the church officials attempt to respond publicly to the scandals of their own personnel, they often make the painful situation worse. For example, five months before the Geoghan affair erupted in January 2002, Christopher Reardon, a lay worker at the Archdiocese of Boston's St. Agnes Church, pleaded guilty to seventy-five counts of criminal molestation of young boys and was sentenced to a prison term of forty to fifty years. The Reardon case elicited sworn testimony before a grand jury that attorneys representing Cardinal Law had encouraged a number of parishioners to keep relevant information from investigators in the hope of forestalling further lawsuits.[38]

The archdiocesan paper, *The Pilot*, in an August 24, 2001, editorial declared that "the accusations that the cardinal ignored, was indifferent to, or refused to address the scandalous behavior of any priest is, at best, ignorant." The editorial went on to say that "no one has suffered more than Cardinal Law" from the abuse of minors at the hands of his priests or diocesan personnel. The point the editorial writer was making is fair and important: the cardinal was and is deeply grieved by the actions of some church personnel against children. To propose that his suffering is no less than the victims and their families is awkward at best and insensitive at worst. Faced with calls for his resignation following the eruption of the Geoghan case and the removal of dozens of priests from their parochial assignments because of previous allegations, Cardinal Law, speaking from his Boston cathedral, said, "When there are problems in the family, you don't walk away. You work them out together with God's help."[39] *The National Review's* editor at large, William F. Buckley, Jr., took the cardinal on:

> The cardinal doesn't understand that one of the problems in the family is the derelict father of the family. It is undeniably and painfully the case that priest after priest who had molested children were called to the cardinal's attention and he did what amounts to nothing. To some he advised, or even decreed, psychological counseling. Others he simply admonished. But the critical concern should have been to get children out of harm's way. He didn't do that. You don't pass over his inactivity as simply an act of inordinate compassion. One can feel with great sorrow and understanding the derangement of the arsonist, but one does not send him back into the forest. Human cordite is otherwise supervised.[40]

For the time being, the church's wounded healers—her priests—struggle on bravely amidst the current storms engulfing the priesthood. The good most priests do in a single day is often remarkable—and overlooked. The harm some do in darkness remains subject to considerable secrecy and denial. The heaviness priests currently bear was captured by Boston's Cardinal Law speaking to his assembled priests just weeks after the first stories of the Geoghan scandal appeared in the press. "I wish it were possible to go back in time and to undo some of the decisions that I made," he said. "I now see that these were wrong decisions. What I have come to learn with a much more vivid clarity during the past weeks is *that our singular focus must be the protection of children* (italics added)."[41]

Cardinal Law might have continued: "[O]ur singular focus must be the protection of children *from our own priests.*"

CHAPTER SEVEN

CLERICAL CULTURE

Clericalism suffocates; it makes part of itself into the whole sacred character of the Church; it makes its power a sacred power to control, to lead, to administer; a power to perform sacraments, and, in general, it makes any power a "power given to me"!

—Alexander Schmemann, *The Journals of Father Alexander Schmemann*

Consecratory power became the obverse of the surrendered sexual power of the celibate so that he could effect a "pure" sacrificial offering. By making priests into new covenant Levites, they became a spiritual caste with their own in-house laws, courts, and clerical preserves.

—Paul E. Dinter, *The Changing Priesthood*

All history shows clearly the hostility of the laity toward the clergy.

—Pope Boniface VIII, *Clericos laicos*

THE YEAR THE SECOND VATICAN COUNCIL ENDED, my ministry as a priest began. With my classmates, I stepped into a priestly culture that seemed firmly grounded and as stable as the church itself. The unspeakable privilege of priesthood made the sacrifice of spouse and children a fair enough price for the new dignity and status I enjoyed as an ordained presbyter. It was too soon after ordination for me to appreciate the wry observation of a wiser, newly ordained priest, "Now that I am a priest, I have a boundless capacity for thwarting good and for turning wine into water." My classmates and I were adjusting to the heady power we now possessed to "confect" the Eucharist—to change bread and wine into the body and blood of Christ—and to forgive sins. We had just been initiated into an elite, worldwide fraternity that destined us to be forever major players in the life of the church and in the battle for souls. Both exhilarated and humbled, we did not know quite how to respond when elderly parishioners tipped their hats and showed us other signs of deference we had yet to earn. These acts of reverence and courtesy, of course, revealed the central role priests played then in the everyday lives of the Catholic faithful.

"Good morning, Father," the cook greeted me as I returned to the rectory after the 6:30 morning Mass, "what would you like for breakfast?" The opportunity for a cooked breakfast each day was one of the more pleasant aspects of rectory living, but certainly not the only one. In addition to prepared meals and laundry and housekeeping service, I regularly enjoyed what my dentist and physician termed "professional courtesies." I was technically living below the poverty line in terms of salary, but living nonetheless like a country gentleman. My basic needs certainly were being met by the rectory staff. There was just enough money to live simply in terms of possessions, but the domestic services, the professional courtesies, and the social status priests enjoyed in that era coalesced to create an overall environment that in most cases was clearly middle class. I lived comfortably, very comfortably.

I loved ministering to the people of St. Christopher's parish in Rocky River, Ohio. The excitement and hope in those first years after the council were tangible. My ministry as preacher and priest, teacher and counselor was demanding but filled with meaning and spiritual energy. Celebrating Mass, especially Sunday Mass, preaching a gospel of grace, hope, and challenge, connecting with people of all ages as they faced the joys and sorrows of everyday living—these were the staples of my life that moved me to profound gratitude and made the loneliness of my celibate world seem like a fair trade-off indeed. Regular visits with family and friends, social outings with classmates and other priests, and invitations to dinner with parishioners provided consistent personal support.

The closing lines of Lacordaires' well-known prayer rang true: "My God, what a life! And it is yours, O Priest of Jesus Christ." I was yet to see that in many ways I was a "prisoner of privilege." The years ahead would reveal the soft underbelly of the clerical culture that so warmly embraced me; a culture that provided for me at a cost I could not fathom in these early years as a priest.

Alexander Schmemann, the Orthodox theologian and seminary dean, writing almost two decades after my 1965 ordination, named the cost that I only suspected was behind the unearned respect that came my way in the first years of my ministry as a priest:

> The tragedy of theological education lies in the fact that young people who seek priesthood are—consciously or unconsciously—seeking this separation, power, this rising above the laity. Their thirst is strengthened and generated by the whole system of theological education, of clericalism. How can they be made to understand, not only with their minds, but their whole being, that one must run away from power, any power, that it is always a temptation . . . ? Christ freed us from that power—"All authority in heaven and on earth has been given to me . . . " (Matthew 28:18)—by revealing the Light of power as power of love, of sacrificial self-offering. Christ gave the Church not "power," but the Holy Spirit . . . In Christ, power returned to God, and man was cured from ruling and commanding.
>
> In the sixty-first year of my life, I suddenly ask myself: How has it all become so perverted? And I become afraid![1]

In the middle 1960s, the clerical culture in which I lived and worked seemed as immutable as the creed itself. It was neither questioned nor critiqued. That such a culture tended to keep priests emotionally immature and excessively dependent on the approval of their superiors and parishioners was yet to be understood. Important work, a certain social status, comfortable quarters, all contributed to a genuine sense of satisfaction for most priests. The patronizing attitude of some parishioners, however, signaled the somewhat less-than-adult standing newly ordained assistant pastors enjoyed in the middle years of the twentieth century.[2] On the one hand, there was no mortgage to pay, no marriage to work at, no children to worry about, and unheard of job security. Priests sensed the envy of some of their married friends. On the other hand, the freedoms that accompanied these exemptions from family responsibilities did not necessarily foster emotional growth.

Without the personal responsibility and the selfless demands required of marriage and parenthood, priests, I came to see, can easily slip into a certain state of self-absorption. Of course, this narcissistic pull is something we all have to deal with and emotional immaturity can be found in adults everywhere, whether married or not, whether paying off mortgages or not. And there are, without question, responsible, integrated, emotionally mature, and spiritually balanced priests too numerous to count. Still, there is evidence that the amorphous, privileged world in which many priests lived then and some still live in now, remains problematic for their own spiritual health, the safety of our young, and the very pastoral mission of the church as well.

Whence the Problem

The negative aspects inherent in clerical culture came into focus as theologians reflected on the nature of the church and the identity of the priest in the years preceding and following Vatican II.[3] Their work, James Whitehead reminds us, revealed a shift in the priest's symbolic position in the community:

> [F]rom the group's unique representative of God (as *alter Christus*) to the leading representative of the group's faith before God . . . . As orchestrator and representative of the community's faith, the priest finds himself in a more intimate relationship with other believers. But he has also lost the privilege and the guaranteed legitimacy that his role once insured. He is compelled to belong to the community in new and unfamiliar ways.[4]

The suspicion takes hold in the heart of the priest that his deepest identity is to be found as a brother among the faithful of God. He may be set apart in one sense as an ecclesial, ordained minister, but he is also set in the midst of the local community as presbyter and servant leader. This new location—the priest's redefined symbolic position in the community—has laid bare the elitist tendencies of the clerical fraternity and seriously undermined the privileges of station mentioned above. It has been a hard pill to swallow for large numbers of priests who perceive the cultural shift as a diminution of the priestly office that in turn is linked to the drop in vocations to the priesthood—a connection we examined at some length in chapter four.

In some clerical circles, efforts to retain the pre-conciliar caste are striking. Long-time friends address each other using their ecclesiastical titles and sporting the latest in clerical vesture. At times the behaviors are manifestly "camp" with the posturing of the dandy.[5] One hears of closed gatherings of seminarians displaying in speech and dress their distinctive identity. The distinction between themselves and the laity is emphasized without reservation. A seminary official approvingly describes such gatherings as fostering not clerical culture, but priestly culture:

> It is odd to observe twenty-somethings trying to act like fifty-somethings. Yet such behavior is found among a small percentage of seminarians today, who gather to drink good scotch, smoke cigars and discuss liturgy (or, more often, liturgical abuses). Cassocks and French cuffs are preferred. A casual observer might wonder if these young men are older than they appear—or simply out of touch with reality. There are also seminarians across the country who gather, somewhat clandestinely, to study papal encyclicals and other works, such as those of St. Thomas Aquinas, which are no longer offered as part of most seminary curricula. There is in all this a hunger for something finer than the best scotch—a hunger for a priestly culture.[6]

Such gatherings, I suspect, represent only a portion of today's newly ordained, many of whom are literally fifty-somethings.

Most see through the posturing and exclusion as somehow working against an inner life rooted in gospel faith and baptismal solidarity with other members of the faithful. Priestly fraternity continues to be important for a healthy and balanced emotional and spiritual life for clergy of all ages. The less clerical, however, and the more fundamentally human that fraternity is, makes all the difference.

One of the problems with dwelling in a less than healthy clerical world is the denial implicit in that world. It is often unspoken but nonetheless present and creates an unnecessary gulf between priest and parishioner. What is worse, it inhibits the kind of social connecting necessary for effective pastoral care and preaching. The unspoken refrain goes something like this: "I am not like the rest of men." Or when gathered with other like-minded priests: "We are not like the rest of men." All this, of course, by the grace of God. Such assumptions, which easily lead to an attitude of entitlement and an exaggerated sense of being special, set the priest up for all manner of falls.

Clericalism

Although clericalism finds its roots in clerical culture, and is intimately linked to it, the distinction should be maintained. Clericalism, as we shall see, is always dysfunctional and haughty, crippling the spiritual and emotional maturity of the priest, bishop, or deacon caught in its web. The laity instinctively resists the patronizing and dominating tendencies in priests who have succumbed to it. While clerical culture is problematic in the ways mentioned above, in itself it is more ambiguous than dysfunctional. It constitutes the world in which clergy live and work, and to a great extent, the world in which they play. It is no more problematic than suburban culture, urban culture, or the culture that defines the work, attitudes, and rituals of the medical profession. Positive and negative aspects are common to each of these cultures and are to be found in clerical culture. Clericalism, on the other hand, involves:

[T]he conscious or unconscious concern to promote the particular interests of the clergy and to protect the privileges and power that have traditionally been conceded to those in the clerical state. There are attitudinal, behavioral and institutional dimensions to the phenomenon of clericalism. Clericalism arises from both personal and social dynamics, is expressed in various cultural forms, and often is reinforced by institutional structures. Among its chief manifestations are an authoritarian style of ministerial leadership, a rigidly hierarchical worldview, and a virtual identification of the holiness and grace of the church with the clerical state and, thereby, with the cleric himself. As such, clericalism is particularly evident in the ordained clergy, though it does not pertain exclusively to it.[7]

Clericalism, as noted here, can be observed at times in nonordained individuals, especially when they are employed at the diocesan or parish levels of the church.[8]

From time to time, in half-joking banter, priests can be heard to say, "Nothing is too good for Father." And on rare occasions these days a parishioner might be heard expressing the same sentiment. The laity, it would seem, have seen the ego-expanding tendencies in such exalted deference more readily than some clerics. For many priests today, even passing, light-hearted references to clerical prerogatives prove uncomfortable. These men are at home with their identity as priests but even more at home with their identity as baptized disciples. Without effort they put others at ease and it is evident that they do not take themselves too seriously. When shown respect they reflect it back to the individual expressing it. They instinctively understand that the priest steeped in clerical posturing weakens a parish's sense of community—and they see community building as one of their primary responsibilities. Without asserting their authority, without the slightest trace of an authoritarian manner, they are perceived by parishioners as profoundly authoritative. The authoritarian priest, on the other hand, even beneath his smooth social glibness, is always angry—and frustrated. Clericalism may command a superficial deference, but it blocks honest human communication and ultimately leaves the cleric practicing it isolated.

Seminarians gathering in French cuffs and tailored cassocks to smoke cigars and sip scotch are already far down the clerical path. Such exclusive meetings of seminarians and priests may indeed build fraternity—but it's the wrong kind. They simply do not foster the pastoral heart parishioners look for in their priests. Women in particular find these kinds of priests off-putting.[9]

Episcopal Clericalism

John L. Allen, Jr., the *National Catholic Reporter*'s Vatican correspondent, reported the following remarks of Australian Bishop David Walker at the 2001 Synod of Bishops on the theme of the episcopacy. Bishop Walker urged his brother bishops to be wary of the influence of a "clerical episcopal subculture." "Bishops who treat people without the normal respect, courtesies and rights that they have rightly come to expect in secular society often go unchecked. Bishops can blatantly ignore their accountability to their priests and people and not be challenged," he said.[10]

A bishop caught up in a clerical style seldom enjoys the kind of fraternal relationship with his priests that both he and they need in order to meet the draining demands of pastoral care and to assuage the burden of loneliness inherent to celibacy. What is worse, episcopal clericalism comes across as arrogance and not infrequently as pompous arrogance. The wisdom and humility of Pope St. Gregory the Great appears lost on a number of the church's prelates. Thomas Cahill writes:

> In regard to his office, [Gregory] retained a wholly admirable humility, infrequent enough in his predecessors, hardly ever displayed by his successors. His favorite title was neither "pope" nor "patriarch of the West," but "servant of the servants of God." He admonished the patriarch of Constantinople for styling himself "the Ecumenical Patriarch" and objected strenuously when the patriarch of Alexandria addressed Gregory as "Universal Papa" (that is, Pope

or Father). "Away with these words," exclaimed the bishop of Rome, "that increase vanity and weaken love!" A bishop should be ever "a minister, not a master," one who attempts "to subdue himself, not his brethren."[11]

Allen went on to report an intriguing suggestion from Ecuadorian Bishop Victor Corral Mantilla who ended his remarks at the synod with an impassioned plea, much in harmony with Gregory the Great, that bishops forgo titles such as "Eminence" and "Excellency" and be called simply "Father." Allen notes that

Cardinal Bernard Agre of Ivory Coast, who happened to be presiding, obviously was not paying careful attention, for when Corral concluded, Agre plunged ahead with the traditional Latin formula of acknowledgment, which goes: "Thank you, Most Excellent Lord."

Laughter was immediate and boisterous, especially when Corral shot back: "You're welcome, Eminence."[12]

The laughter, I am afraid, muted a significant proposal that deserved serious consideration. Bishop Corral's intervention led me to imagine a post-Pentecost discussion among Jesus' apostles. The twelve, sensing the important implications of apostolic succession, thought it reasonable to propose appropriate titles for the exalted office of "bishop." James suggests "Your Eminence" as worthy of their station. Matthias thinks "Your Grace" has a nice ring to it, Andrew likes "Your Excellency," and Thomas indicates his pleasure with "My Lord" (Monsignor). The discussion turns serious, even solemn, until Mary of Nazareth and Mary Magdalene, present but silent to this point, intervene. They say not a word, but their eyes meet the eyes of each of the apostles who have grown quiet. Under the gaze of the two women, the apostles color in embarrassment. Each knows in his heart how the Master would respond to their deliberations.

Titles carried over from feudal and courtly ages long past tend to overshadow our fundamental, common identity in the Body of Christ. They are the hallmarks of clericalism.

Clerical Ambition

A priest psychologist I know and respect once made an off-handed remark that caught me up short. Ambition, he said, is as much a fundamental human instinct as sexuality. But like sex, priests and religious aren't supposed to have any of it. I remember asking a bright, devout young man once if he ever thought about being a priest, adding that I thought he had what it takes to be a very good one. He responded without hesitation, "No, I don't want to be a priest, I want to be a bishop."

His candor was refreshing. But truth be told, a large number of priests and seminarians would like nothing better than to be named a bishop. Especially in the celibate world of the Latin rite, nothing quite pleases the soul as the realization that one is thought well of by one's superiors. There are, of course, few human rewards in the priesthood—limited opportunities for promotion, occasional small salary increases, little public acclaim other than perhaps being made a monsignor. In the clerical world, which is fundamentally still a feudal world, a priest needs to capture the eye of his bishop if he is to find what the British refer to as a "preferment." And because ambition, like sex, is thought in church circles to be unseemly, its urgent longings must be carefully guarded and disguised. A thoughtful note or a tastefully chosen gift to the priest's ecclesial superior may really be motivated by ambitious longings the priest himself has more or less successfully repressed.

In this climate, the ambitious priest is keenly sensitive to the effect an imprudent word might have on his ecclesial career. What his superiors might think is often the defining factor that shapes his speech and behavior. Such a priest surrenders his intellectual life, no longer thinking theologically or pastorally with any kind of creativity or imagination. His principal virtues become unthinking obedience and a rigid orthodoxy and his behavior is always that of the proper clergyman.

A skilled spiritual director capable of seeing the implications of such skewed ambition would point out to the priest how easy it is to identify institutional rewards, with their trappings and power, with divine approval. Approval—divine and human—and the personal validation that follows rest at the core of clerical ambition. Power, of course, is always attractive, even seductive. But in the feudal, clerical culture in which many priests still live, move, and work, it is often the approving nod of the bishop, his warm glance, that is the ultimate reward. This wordless gesture personifies a courtly decorum of centuries past and hints at yet unnamed future rewards. The secret delight taken in the patron's nod is sweet indeed, but its price is diminishment of soul. Here style takes precedence over substance, deferential agreement over honest conversation. The priest returns to his room less capable of living his own life with passion and integrity.[13]

A number of bishops have understood the psychological and spiritual pitfalls of clerical culture and have moved to offset them. These bishops signal their priests that they are their elder brother rather than their all-knowing and all-wise "father." They create a spirit in the presbyterate that fosters adult responsibility and open discussion of issues that really matter. In such a climate their priests breathe fresh air and discover that their deepest ambition is to be the disciple and priest God has called them to be. This holy ambition for union with God—and union with their sisters and brothers in Christ—shapes and colors their entire priestly ministry. And their parishioners sense that their pastors are good and holy men.

Unfortunately, bishops with their own ambition problems strive and maneuver for more prestigious dioceses. Such episcopal ambition, acknowledged publicly by Cardinals Joseph Ratzinger, prefect of the Congregation for the Doctrine of the Faith, and Bernard Gautin, former prefect of the Congregation for Bishops, appears commonplace. Ambitious bishops, not surprisingly, keep alive the older, closed clerical system with its subtle protocols for advancement and recognition. In such a system neither human sexuality nor human ambition can be discussed openly and honestly. In place of such candid conversation, the ambitious priest protests too much that he is neither sexual nor ambitious. A note of unreality takes hold and, as the spiritual masters of our tradition remind us, the grace of God dwells only in that which is real. Unholy ambition in a priest is always a signal that his faith is weak. His belief in dogmas and doctrinal statements from the Vatican may indeed be strong, but his ecclesial careerism gives him away. He has yet to take the gospel to heart. He has yet to discover what really matters.

Unhealthy ambition is but one of the faces of clerical culture. It is a symptom of a system that is sick and in need of healing. Repressed ambition, like repressed sexuality, eventually erupts in behaviors and attitudes that demoralize and scandalize the faithful. It will be with the church as long as its present structures are assumed to be above review and renewal.

CHAPTER EIGHT

GAY MEN IN THE PRIESTHOOD

If this estimate is close to the truth [50% of priests and seminarians have a homosexual orientation], then half of all our priests and seminarians are being recruited from roughly 5 to 8 percent of the general population of American Catholic men. This is a very sobering statistic.

—Robert J. Egan, *Commonweal*

Since most men have a woman to love, whom is the gay man to love? God, surely, in the context of community and a noble, celibate service. This is the pattern of history, for then the sexual is absorbed in the loving communion with God and community.

—Matthew Kelty, Trappist monk and author

It is my conviction that gays make superb celibates, the best celibates, the more so in community. I do not think the heterosexually oriented man should try to live celibacy.

—Matthew Kelty

I RAISED THIS ISSUE as carefully and respectfully as I could in *The Changing Face of the Priesthood.*[1] No topic received more affirmation than did my discussion of the large numbers of homosexually oriented men in our seminaries and presbyterates. Both gay and straight priests told me the issue needed to be placed on the table. Nor did any topic in the book receive more criticism and denial—strident, harsh, and sometimes hysterical—than did the issue of a strong gay subculture in our seminaries, chanceries, and rectories. It was read as an attack on the priesthood. Some priests, seminarians, and laity contested the estimates I reported of the number of gay men in our seminaries and rectories. Privately, I was told by a number of bishops who were in seminary work before being named to the episcopacy that the estimates I quoted matched their own experience of the gay/straight ratio. Consider theologian Mark Jordan's assessment:

> Everyone seems to agree that there are now more homosexuals in the Catholic priesthood and religious life than the population at large. This is hardly surprising. The priesthood and religious life are all-male institutions that reward vows of celibacy within a religion that demands celibacy of all homosexuals. If you have to be celibate anyway, why not get rewarded for it—and do it in the company of other men with similar inclinations?[2]

From the perspective of secrecy and denial and their implications for sound theological reflection concerning homosexuality, Jordan argues that the actual percentage of gay seminarians, religious, and priests is not the place to focus our attention:

> If we are trying to determine how closets are constructed in the Catholic church, how they inhibit theological thinking about homosexuality, the exact percentage of gay priests is really beside the point. It doesn't much matter whether it is 5 percent or 25 percent or 50 percent. The construction and enforcement of rules of silence will operate at any of those levels, because the closet is a collaborative construction of gay and straight. The strength of the system of secrecy doesn't depend on the number of gay people who are having sex in secret. It depends on the number of those who are afraid of that secret sex, about which they may know only what their own fears or fantasies whisper. There may be just one homosexually active monsignor in a curial office of ten, but the closet around him is built by all ten together, without anyone saying a word. That is why there is no easy correlation between a higher percentage of gay clergy and better conditions of visibility. The recent increase in the perceived number of gay clergy has opened some closet doors, but it has locked others more securely.[3]

If I read Jordan correctly, what sustains the silence and reinforces the closet is fear, whether the fear of the gay priest about his own orientation and possible discovery, the fear of the straight priest to see what he really does not want to see and to incorporate this knowledge into his understanding of clerical culture, or the fear of the ambivalent priest who suspects, to his own horror, that he may be gay. The criticism directed at *The Changing Face of the Priesthood* was almost exclusively focused on the chapter dealing with gay priests, religious, and seminarians. And in light of Jordan's analysis, it was rooted in fear rather than rational disagreement about the various estimates of gay seminarians and priests that were cited.

Clearly, I had touched a nerve. I had dared to explore one of the most taboo of issues facing the church and, in particular, clerical culture. Nowhere, I came to see, is the theme of this present book more exemplified than in the deeply entrenched denial and carefully maintained silence surrounding the important issue of sexual orientation and clerical life. Speaking of the so-called "pink palace" seminaries, one diocesan official remarked, "Everybody knows it has been a problem. . . . But you can't say that officially, because it will blow up in your face."[4]

There are other factors at work maintaining the silence. Church leaders are reluctant to address clergy sexual misconduct in general. For example, missionaries report large numbers of priests in Latin America and Africa who have fathered children and live in clandestine, and not so clandestine, relationships. In some countries the sexually active priests are clearly the majority of the clergy. These same church leaders, I suspect, deny overwhelming evidence that celibacy is not being practiced because it might lead to questions about the wisdom and viability of mandatory celibacy for the Latin rite. Better, it is thought, to deny the widespread nonobservance than to admit that it simply is not working.

Concerning the church's denial of homosexuality and homosexual activity in the priesthood, some attribute the silence to a "discreet but powerful homosexual network within seminaries and chanceries."[5] Bound together by their common knowledge of sexual activity within and beyond the group, there appears little anxiety that their secret social life will be exposed. The network at times is expanded when a priest becomes sexually involved with a seminarian or younger priest. As the senior priest moves into ever-more important diocesan positions, he brings the junior priest along on his coattails.[6] The younger priest enjoys the influence of a "patron," but at a considerable price—the loss of his integrity if not his soul. It is also a dangerous game for the patron; both he and his protégé are susceptible to blackmail. The 1999 case of Santa Rosa Bishop Patrick Ziemann is but one example. Ziemann acknowledged a sexual relationship with one of his priests, but insisted it was consensual. The priest, however, claimed he was blackmailed into having a sexual liaison with his bishop.[7]

When priests in such networks attain leadership posts, the health and morale of the presbyterate itself are at stake. I suspect a good number of these networks are celibate in the sense that there is little or no sexual contact among its members. Priests and seminarians in these loosely structured groups find the company of other like-minded men spiritually and aesthetically enriching. They share, nonetheless, a common secret—the existence of their gay world and the joy they find in it. The secret inevitably reinforces the network and its excluding power. The effect even of celibate networks on seminaries and presbyterates is unhealthy and divisive. They reinforce a culture of secrecy.

While the wall of denial and silence appears firmly buttressed, there are signs that it is weakening and might, sooner rather than later, buckle. And as the walls come down there is evidence that some aspects of the gay culture are discovering a fresh liberation in celibate chastity. In the April 2002 issue of *Out* magazine, for example, Brad Gooch writes about his thirty-year fascination with celibacy, monasticism, and homosexuality. In his twenties and living in Paris as a grad student, Gooch discovered he was serious both about celibacy and monasticism. His interest in "cowls and vows"—in celibate, homoerotic communal living—led him on a

spiritual journey to numerous communities including an Episcopal monastery and the famous Abbey of Gethsemani in Kentucky.
After a morning run with a brother from the Episcopal monastery, his running partner made a pass. Gooch writes:

> Sensing my surprise, he explained that another monk was actually
> his lover but that he was away for a month. My surprise only
> deepening at his explanation, he filled me in on the reinterpreta-
> tion within his community of the monastic vow of "chastity" as
> stressing "integrity" rather than "celibacy." I resonated happily
> enough with this "love the one you're with" attitude, though I de-
> clined the offer—being self-righteously opposed in those days to
> "cheating" (not on God, on the boyfriend).[8]

At Gethsemani, Gooch found a more traditional understanding of
celibacy influencing the chastity of the gay monks he met. Now,
decades later, he was revisiting a number of the monasteries that
offered hospitality to him when he was on his youthful quest. He
notes a significant difference:

> The big change was that most with whom I spoke now embraced
> chastity and its usual marker—celibacy—as an appealing aspect of
> the life. Some had entered in middle age after active romantic lives
> in major urban centers. Others who stayed behind when their
> brothers departed in the '70s had thought through their decisions
> and resolved to embrace rather than dismiss. Of course, by speak-
> ing positively about chastity and celibacy as a way of life, all of
> them were presenting a challenge to any gays who feel that the
> acting out of their sexuality is their identity.[9]

We need to hear more from mature, integrated gay monks and
priests. For the most part they remain invisible, painfully aware
that their bishops and superiors steadfastly deny that they exist in
abundance in our rectories and monasteries—and equally aware
that most bishops are unwilling to tolerate any public acknowledgment of their orientation. By silencing these mature gay voices,
the church is denied their witness as faithful and brave priests and

religious. In doing so the church also sustains the deeply held belief that gay priests and religious are somehow damaged goods. Of
course, nothing would hasten the crumbling of the walls of secrecy more than healthy, celibate, and faithful gay bishops acknowledging their orientation. In the present state of the church,
however, such testimony would demand heroic moral courage.

Recent scholarly studies addressing the church and homosexuality offer careful, honest analyses of why the walls of silence are,
in spite of some obvious crumbling, so fiercely maintained. Among
them are Mark Jordan's *The Silence of Sodom: Homosexuality in
Modern Catholicism,* James Alison's *Faith Beyond Resentment:
Fragments Catholic and Gay,* and Ellis Hanson's *Decadence and Catholicism.*[10] Jordan's work is a compelling philosophical-historical-
moral treatise; Alison's is a fresh theological and anthropological
reflection; and Hanson's is a sometimes tedious work exploring the
relationship between homoeroticism and Catholicism in late-
nineteenth-century aesthetes. Each of these books reflects careful
scholarship from a common perspective. Readers, I suspect, will
find them provocative and, especially in the case of Jordan's and
Hanson's works, controversial. Yet each in its own manner is an invitation to go beyond the fearful silence and to engage in honest,
respectful dialogue about this important issue. Other voices from
different perspectives would balance and strengthen the conversation. As Jordan rightly observes, "I am convinced that we need to
speak about these things [gay priests] not only for the abstract
sake of honesty, but for the real and concrete motive of resisting
the effects of closeted homosexuality in church bureaucracies."[11]

Jordan and Alison name the real issue—closeted homosexuality. And they explore the fallout closeted homosexuality inevitably
breeds: institutional homophobia and the violence it renders upon
the gay priest, religious, and seminarian; a homoeroticized clerical
culture; a stunting of honest, creative, theological thinking about
the Catholic understanding of sexuality in general and homosexuality in particular. In *The Changing Face of the Priesthood* I addressed the implications of a closeted homosexuality for seminary

formation, proposing that straight seminarians feel destabilized in environments that have significant numbers of gay seminarians.[12] The seminary world would be considerably healthier, I hold, for the straight, gay, and confused seminarian, if gay students felt free to acknowledge their orientation to the seminary rector and formation faculty. Presbyterates would be healthier if gay priests felt comfortable in discussing their sexuality with their bishop. Their orientation should not be the defining characteristic of their inner world or their social world. A culture that fosters closeted homosexuality—a "don't ask, don't tell" culture—is by definition unhealthy. It impedes the spiritual journey of the priest or seminarian and violates the integrity of his soul. Orientation is not something one should be ashamed of. In spite of church documents to the contrary, shame is precisely what many gay priests, religious, and seminarians feel.

At least let them listen carefully to the advice of William McDonough:

> I am not arguing here for public disclosure of sexual identity by gay clergy. I am looking for a twofold acknowledgment, one that is public and one that is personal. At the level of public discourse in the church, I am advocating the general acknowledgment that there are a significant number of homosexually oriented, celibate men in the priesthood. At the personal level I am suggesting something perhaps more costly to those directly affected: that homosexually oriented priests acknowledge at least to themselves the reality of their orientation.[13]

Priests Dying of AIDS

In late January 2000, journalist Judy L. Thomas rocked the U.S. Catholic Church with a front page, three-part series in *The Kansas City Star* reporting that hundreds of priests had died of AIDS-related illnesses and that hundreds more were infected with the virus that causes the disease. Cries of denial were heard immediately from the National Conference of Catholic Bishops and from pulpits from coast to coast. The cries were accompanied in many cases with attacks on Thomas and *The Star* for attacking the Catholic faith.

Ten months later, Thomas reported that *The Star* had documented through death certificates and interviews with family members and colleagues more than three hundred AIDS-related priest deaths. She noted that because death certificates are closed in nearly two-thirds of the states, the exact number of AIDS-related deaths among Catholic clergy is impossible to tally. It is reasonable to assume that the number is higher, significantly higher, than the three hundred reported. Moreover, "*The Star* found that the AIDS death rate among priests was more than double that of all adult males in those states [with open access to death certificates] and more than six times that of the general population in those states."[14] According to Richard Selik, a medical epidemiologist and AIDS expert with the Centers for Disease Control and Prevention in Atlanta, "The available data shows that the HIV death rate is higher among priests than it is in the general population of men 25 and older."[15]

The denial, nevertheless, remained constant. In a number of the larger U.S. dioceses, dioceses with four hundred to five hundred priests, the number of priests that had died of AIDS was often four or five—one out of one hundred, a figure giving credibility to *The Star* series. Yet the word from diocesan spokespersons echoed the prevailing official stance: only a small number of priests were homosexually oriented and only a very small percentage of priests were sexually active. Church officials themselves stood guard at the closet doors.

The Straight Subculture

In spite of feverish efforts to keep closet doors closed, the current torrent of clergy abuse scandals and the concomitant unraveling of clerical culture focus attention on the issue of sexual orientation. As the closet doors of our rectories and seminaries creep open, we are likely to discover that the real subculture is not gay, after all, but straight. According to Mark Jordan, Ellis Hanson, and others, there is sufficient evidence to believe that this is indeed the situation in many, if not most, of our seminaries, religious congregations of men, and our diocesan assemblies of priests.[16] The same pattern is seen in allegations of sexual abuse brought against bishops. Bishop Zieman, Bishop Symons, Bishop O'Connell, Archbishop Platz, Cardinal Gröer, come to mind. And the recent Vatican directives mentioned above forbidding the admission of homosexually oriented candidates to seminary formation programs reflects the official church's concern that there is an orientation problem in our seminaries.

While the Geoghan case in Boston has laid bare the multilayered tragedy of priest pedophilia, the more common boundary violation of minors by clergy remains, not pedophilia, but the sexual abuse of postpubescent, teenage boys. Because the number of teenage girls victimized by priest abusers is dramatically lower than the number of teenage boys abused, many commentators see a link between sexual orientation and clergy abuse of adolescent minors.[17] Especially when asexual religious, priests, and bishops (individuals who manifest no sexual energy or interest whatsoever) are added to the mix, the suspicion grows that the true subculture in our seminaries, chanceries, rectories, and religious houses is not gay, but straight.

Scapegoating the Celibate Gay Priest

Caught at the center of the worst scandal they have ever known, most priests lean into the storm and bravely carry on. Whether straight or gay, priests cope as best they can with the stress and discouragement that now accompanies their daily efforts to meet the pastoral demands of a growing U.S. Catholic population with the ever thinning, ever aging clerical ranks. Since *The Boston Globe* broke the John Geoghan case in January 2002, priests find their stress level skyrocketing and their once unquestioned authority plummeting as they stand, chilled and grieving, at the center of arguably the worst scandal ever to rock the U.S. church.

Gay priests, moreover, in the public eye as never before, brace themselves for anti-gay assaults. And Catholics, sitting at their kitchen tables, discuss the role homosexuality plays in the abuse of teenage boys. They wonder how the current attention on homosexuality and abuse will affect the priesthood and the church itself.

The focus of the scandal triggered in the Boston Archdiocese moved from the tragic, unspeakable harm done to thousands of children and teens by Catholic priests to the incomprehensible bungling of numerous bishops dealing with local scandals: reassignment of abuser priests—sometimes with positive testimonials—to unsuspecting parishes and dioceses; secret cash settlements with broken promises by church officials not to give abuser priests access to minors; and hardball legal tactics against abuse victims by diocesan attorneys. Gradually, another element of the scandal came into focus.

As report after report received almost daily front-page coverage in papers from coast to coast, an important clinical distinction finally received the attention it deserved. Most priest abusers were not pedophiles—adults who find their sexual drives almost exclusively directed toward prepubescent boys and girls. Rather they fell into the category of ephebophiles (from *ephebeus,* one of the Greek nouns for a postpubescent youth). Both pedophilia and ephebophilia are criminal, and in the eyes of most religious traditions, immoral. As the distinction took hold in the minds of parishioners and the general public, a disturbing phenomenon to the abuse scandal came into focus: most reported victims of priest abusers were teenage boys. While some therapists and researchers disputed this profile of the typical victim citing the large numbers of cases that remain unreported—especially of adult women—the consensus holds when cases of teenagers abused by priests are reviewed.

Why, it is reasonable to ask, are there so few teenage girls among the victims? While difficult to answer at the present time with any kind of clinical precision, the predominance of male teenage victims raised the issue addressed by Richard McBrien and Andrew Greeley almost fifteen years ago—the presence of significant numbers of homosexually oriented men in the priesthood.[18]

Again and again, commentators and behavioral specialists have stressed the absence of any link between pedophilia, celibacy, and sexual orientation, noting that most pedophiles are married men. Not surprising, of course, since there are many more married men in our population than celibate priests. But the point remains of critical importance in the present discussion: it is wrong to link sexual orientation, specifically a gay orientation, with the abuse of children. Still, we need to probe the significance of the disproportionate number of teenage boys among the victims of nonpedophile priest abusers. Before turning to that issue and the presence of large numbers of gay men in the priesthood, some contextual considerations are in order.

Holy and Gay

Like their straight brothers, gay priests comprise a continuum from the very gifted to the moderately gifted, from the mature and healthy to the immature and pathological, from the hardworking to the well rested, and from men of authentic holiness to charlatans using the priesthood as a cover to meet their own needs and desires. Most, of course, are found not at the polar ends of the continuum, but somewhere in the middle range of these scales. But, without question, there are gay priests of extraordinary spiritual depth and vitality. These men minister quietly and effectively and sometimes heroically as did Fr. Mychal Judge who died ministering to firefighters at the World Trade Center.

Like their straight brothers, gay priests speak quietly of the profound sadness that crowds their working day and disturbs their sleep as well. They know that everything is different now in light of the 2002 abuse scandals which shook the foundations of the priesthood and the church itself. As young priests they stood on the shoulders of pastors who went before them receiving trust and respect they themselves had never earned in the least. That pre-won trust and respect, they fear, is mostly gone now. From time to time, priests catch hints of wariness and suspicion in their parishioners. "You can trust me," they want to say. "Your children are safe with me." Along with the victims and their families, priests understand they have their own grief work to do. And in their darker moments, they wonder what kind of legacy they will leave the priests that came after them.

In today's church it's prudent for gay priests to remain hidden. They hear talk show guests and read op/ed writers raising the issue of homosexuals in the priesthood, pointing to the teenage male victims preferred by priest abusers. Many celibate gay priests feel like scapegoats.

Coping with the suspicion priests in general were feeling—plus the added suspicion focused on gay priests—gay clergy often find themselves ministering to victims betrayed by colleagues. Some of the abuser priests are their friends and seminary classmates. They know their parents and their considerable achievements. Now they see a dark side they never suspected. With their straight colleagues, they apologize again and again for the sins of their brother priests but sense the limitations of their words in the face of so many other words that were later seen as lies. With the Catholic faithful, they long for a healthier, holier priesthood.

Most gay priests, I believe, live with another level of pain and conflict that is only minimally understood, even by their families and friends. Their church teaches that a homosexual orientation is an objective disorder. Does that mean the church holds that they *as persons* are objectively disordered? No, but this fine distinction is of little comfort from an existential point of view. Can objectively disordered people be really holy? Lead lives of genuine sanctity? Without question, but sexual identity is so central to a fundamental sense of self that it is an easy step to conclude that a gay individual himself or herself is "objectively disordered."

So most continue to minister, conflicted but faithful, on behalf of a church that teaches they are "God's beloved sons" but nevertheless objectively disordered insofar as their orientation is concerned—an orientation they never chose nor sought.

As men of the church, they are expected to uphold this teaching and bring it to the attention of the gay and lesbian parishioners they counsel. They listen to the parents of gay children who wonder if they did something wrong in raising their gay son or lesbian daughter, all the while keeping their own orientation secret. They read and hear about straight seminarians leaving their studies for the priesthood because of the influence of gay subcultures in houses of formation. The exiting straight seminarians report they felt like outsiders, unable to feel at home and at ease. I've seen gay priests nod at such reports. Often they are sympathetic but they themselves know only too keenly what it is like to be a gay priest in a church that judges their orientation to be objectively disordered. They believe they know more than most what it is like to be an outsider.

Gay priests wince when they hear Vatican leaders like Archbishop Tarcisio Bertone of the Congregation for the Doctrine of the Faith say that gay men should not be admitted to the priesthood. Closer to home, Philadelphia's Cardinal Anthony Bevilacqua asserted that gay men were not suitable for the priesthood, even if they were committed to a celibate life. "By his [the gay candidate's] orientation," the cardinal said, "he's not giving up family and marriage. He's giving up what the church considers an aberration, a moral evil."[19] (Does Cardinal Bevilacqua mean to imply that gay men who are not sexually active are less chaste than straight men who are not sexually active?) Bishop John D'Arcy of Fort Wayne-South Bend also echoed Archbishop Bertone's position: "I'm convinced that (the priesthood) should be limited to men who are heterosexual. . . . I'm going to get criticized for that. I don't think it's fair to a person with a homosexual orientation to put him into a life, that for the most part, they cannot handle."[20] Along with gay priests, many gay and straight Catholics found the position of Archbishop Bertone and Bishop D'Arcy confounding. If the church requires all homosexually oriented individuals to lead lives of celibacy why, they ask, is it unwilling to welcome gay candidates for the priesthood? Is celibacy in the priesthood more difficult than celibacy in the world?

With more than a hint of cynicism, gays and others wonder, "Isn't it interesting that God is calling so many objectively disordered individuals to the priesthood."

Like most Catholics, gay priests were dismayed when they read in March 2002 that Vatican spokesman Joaquin Navarro-Valls questioned the very validity of ordination of homosexually oriented priests, proposing, in effect, that gay priests are not really priests at all. The assertion, regarded as absurd in most church circles, led commentators to speculate on the number of priests and bishops who would be counted among the "invalidly" ordained. If gay priests and bishops were indeed to be drummed out of the ministry, the sacramental life of the church would be brought dangerously close to collapse.

The Dark Side of Gay

Some bishops will admit privately that they know of some gay priests—and some straight clergy—who have rationalized celibacy to mean little more than not marrying. Romantic liaisons and sexual encounters, whether in the context of a committed relationship or of a more casual nature, are considered acceptable.

If celibate gay priests deserve support and acceptance, sexually active gay priests, like sexually active straight priests, deserve to be challenged. Sadly, examples of the shadow side of gay clerical life abound. Gay laymen report seeing priests at gay bars and guests at gay parties. Most, in their view, are looking for more than relaxing conversation. Internet chat rooms for gay clergy are reported and priests are observed visiting gay adult video and bookstores. Worst of all, sex rings are uncovered at orphanages run by religious orders.

Stories of seduction are numerous now. And while clergy abuse of adults reveals a preponderance of women victims, the abuse of teenagers, as we have noted, remains focused on young males. Some of these victims of abuse—and some abusers themselves—report they were seduced while seminarians by seminary faculty. We read of priests taking teenage boys to Rome, including visits with the pope, and nightmare nights of abuse; of "wrestling matches" in rectory basements; of bizarre initiations into secret, all-male, priest-led clubs. And the link between teen abuse and gay priests is reinforced. Occasionally, sexually active gay priests can be heard invoking classical Greek and Latin authors who celebrated man-boy relationships that included sexual relations. Others behave as if their only responsibility is to be discreet, admitting to hundreds of sexual encounters. Almost all, they admit, were anonymous.

Celibate priests, gay and straight, know from personal experience the struggle involved in remaining chaste. Most are forgiving when faced with their own and their brothers' occasional failures. They don't understand, however, the cavalier attitude of some priests who believe discretion is their only responsibility. Faced with the abuse of children and teens by their brother priests, they are livid.

As pastors they try to understand. They find some solace as a profile emerges of clergy who abuse minors. They are lonely men—sexually conflicted, psychosexually immature, and lacking the skills and self-knowledge necessary for meaningful adult friendships. From a psychological perspective, they remain teenagers themselves looking for experiences of intimacy that prove tragic for their victims and disastrous for their own spiritual lives. Some simply exploit their privileged access to teens. Others, it appears, are true predators able to move skillfully in varied and different social circles while stalking their intended victims.

Facing the Real Issue

It's common knowledge now. Some straight priests cross the line with adult women and girls in their teens. Some gay priests cross the line with adult men and with boys in their teens. In the cases of adult women and men, the behavior is immoral. When the victims are teenage boys and girls, the behavior is immoral—and criminal. The extent of the scandal reveals how simplistic and dishonest are attempts to explain these tragic abuses of trust as an example of a few bad apples in an otherwise healthy barrel.

Something more complex is at the bottom of these behaviors. Priest perpetrators live in a closed, all-male system of privilege, exemption, and secrecy that drives sexuality underground. There, deprived of light, sexual impulses easily become twisted and sick. Gary Wills is right to point to the role mandated celibacy plays in the abuse of minors and the church's now failed attempts to cover-up the scandals.[21] There is something wrong, Catholics and others now see, with the clerical system itself—a closed system of legislated celibacy, hierarchical accountability, and feudal privilege. The system requires serious review by lay leaders, priests, bishops, and the Vatican, if the church is to regain its moral voice and credibility.

The priesthood desperately needs fresh air and the light of a spring morning. But the shutters remain, for the most part, closed. The drastic drop in seminary enrollments prompt some church leaders to keep the priesthood's crisis in the dark out of fear that a bad situation will be made worse. The opposite, of course, is true. The priesthood, like the clergy of most mainline religions, is undergoing a crisis that includes but goes beyond the issue of orientation. Yet sexual orientation is likely the most complex and sensitive of the factors at work here. Now is the time for the church to address with compassion and sensitivity a reality it wants to deny: many of its priests and bishops are gay.

Coming to grips with this reality is a critical first step to a renewed church and a healthier priesthood.

CHAPTER NINE

MINISTRY AND LEADERSHIP

I know . . . that the great prejudice against the Church among educated Englishmen is not a religious one against dogmas, but an ethical and political one; they think that no Catholic can be truthful, honest or free, and that if he tries to be he is subject to persecution.

—Lord Acton

Thank God the vocation crisis is over.

—A U.S. Cardinal Archbishop

SINCE JANUARY 2002 the reality and scope of clergy sexual abuse against children and teenagers have forever changed not only the face of the priesthood but the very face of the church. Layer upon layer of denial and silence continue to be pulled away, revealing wounds and weapons that demand attention. The wounds of the clergy's victims demand the best healing efforts of the church's leaders and ministers. Figuratively and literally, bishops need to find ways to wash the feet of abuse victims and to dry their tears. In actions that confound the cynical, and in spite of lingering pain, some abuse victims are ministering to the very bishops responsible for reassigning abuser priests. They whisper their forgiveness and silently bless church authorities who were more concerned about avoiding scandal than stopping abuse.

The weapons of silence and denial are slowly being turned into plowshares—sadly, less by responsible action on the part of church leaders than by the courageous initiative of the victims themselves, supported by family, friends, and members of their parish communities. Reacting to the pleas of victims given new voice by a steady stream of media reports of clergy abuse, the church no longer remains silent and quietly, one hopes, reflects on its own tendency to denial and minimization. When the church, however, does speak of its concern and sympathy for victims and their families, it sometimes betrays its pastoral sentiments by employing legal strategies and deposition tactics that have upset and angered victims and parishioners alike.[1] It gives the impression that it sees any request for cash settlements or any legal action taken against the church as a decision on the part of the victim and his attorney to play "hardball." Church officials appear to think they are justified in using hardball tactics in response to what they consider to be the hardball tactics of victims and their attorneys. The effects of such assumptions on the part of church authorities have compounded the pain and suffering of victims. The damage done to the church's image when such power tactics are employed is considerable.

Without question, the "troubles" that erupted in January 2002 have sullied the reputation of both bishops and priests, the ordained ministers of the church.[2] In such a climate, where do Catholics turn when some of their pastors and bishops have failed to protect their children from the abuse of other pastors and bishops? They turn, I believe, to their fellow Catholics, to members of their parish community, to neighbors and friends whose goodness and compassion are beyond question. They speak to these "ministers" of their pain and anger, of their disillusionment with much of the institutional church, of their profound sense of betrayal. And in speaking to their fellow believers they discover that all believers have the God-given grace to be wounded healers. And they are comforted. Soon they come to see that the community itself, *the faithful themselves*, are ministers of healing and mercy.

Where the church's official ministers have failed, the church as people has responded with healing words and signs of concern that reveal the abiding presence of God. Many Catholics, precisely because of the abuse scandals, discover, as if for the first time, that they are indeed brothers and sisters in Christ. The Spirit's true healers, they discover, are to be found everywhere, not just in those officially delegated to staff parishes and church institutions. It is found in mothers and fathers whose children have been abused, in grandparents numbed with confusion and heartache, in coworkers and lay leaders ready to offer support and friendship. This legacy of grace can be seen stirring the hearts of ordinary Catholics of all stripes to meet the ministerial crisis gripping the church. Such an awakening is one of the signs of the Spirit working in the midst of the present troubles.

Even as parishioners accept their responsibility to minister to one another as their gifts and skills allow, the church remains faced with a perilous situation in terms of parochial ministry in general and priestly ministry in particular. In spite of the emerging contrite face of the church, now at least partially visible in the wake of un-precedented abuse scandals, the church's official statements about ministry at the turn of the century remain, inexplicably, optimistic. Consider the remark of a cardinal archbishop to his priests in 2000, "Thank God the vocation crisis is finally over." A far more realis-tic assessment comes from Austrian Bishop Reinhold Stecher:

> Not long ago a bishop renowned for his conservatism said to me with a smile: "In our diocese every priest has three parishes—and things run splendidly." That most reverend gentleman has never had the responsibility for even one parish—let alone three. If he had, he could hardly have made such a lighthearted remark. In France I have met worn-out, exhausted priests who have to attend to seven or even ten parishes. Even if such priests have the best theological qualifications, their voices will never be heard in the Church's higher councils. Such priests are not made bishops. Few bishops know what these priests face—with the result that their experiences and frustrations are never represented at the Church's highest level. The best we bishops can do is to sigh sympathetically about the difficulties our priests face and utter moving complaints about the shortage of Christian families capable of producing celi-bate vocations. At a higher level still all energies are devoted to de-fending the existing rules. . . . The Church's real needs are never

considered. . . . The tendency to place human laws and traditions above our divine commission is the most shocking aspect of many church decisions at the end of this millennium.[3]

Somehow, the official church believes it will manage to meet the pastoral and sacramental needs of parishioners with its present corps of priest, religious, and lay ministers. It is clear there still exists in numerous quarters of the church considerable denial about the drastic challenge facing the church's ministers at the turn of the century.

In an effort to at least partially rend the present curtain of denial surrounding the future of ministry, we examine here the more basic realities that continue to be minimized and, in some cases, denied. This may, it is hoped, permit a more realistic glimpse at the face of ministry in the years ahead.

Brave Hearts

Before examining the critical numerical evidence defining the present state of ministry, a word about the ministers themselves. Ministers staffing the contemporary parish not only include priests, religious, and deacons, but also lay ministers, especially women lay ministers. The latter category represents a dramatic shift in the profile of parochial ministers—Catholic ministry is no longer identified solely with the ministrations of the priest.

These parochial ministers and their episcopal confreres, especially in urban and missionary environs, and in developing countries, often minister at considerable, personal risk. In El Salvador, for example, Archbishop Oscar Romero witnessed the murder of dozens of his priests before he himself was assassinated for challenging the injustice of the reigning political powers. Maryknoll sisters Maura Clarke and Ita Ford, Ursuline sister Dorothy Kazel and lay missionary Jean Donovan were abducted outside San Salvador's airport in 1980, taken to a secluded area, raped, and murdered. In November 1989, six Jesuits from the University of Central America, their housekeeper, and her daughter, were brutally killed by government soldiers. Preaching the gospel and ministering in the gospel's name, inevitably makes enemies and places ministers in harm's way, whether in Central or South America, or the more affluent cities of the world. The heroic death of Fr. Mychal Judge at the World Trade Center on September 11, 2001, recalls the heroism of military chaplains who gave their lives in the major wars of the last century as well as missionaries and ministers who daily serve in dangerous environs.

Easily overlooked, however, is the moral bravery of countless ministers who serve God's people with unwavering commitment. Often alone, overworked and stretched to the point of exhaustion, they carry on without much attention or appreciation. These women and men know that ministering in the name of the gospel is not for the fainthearted. And they understand better than most that the picture is likely to get worse before it gets better. Lay ministry, it appears, will continue to expand in the foreseeable future as the number of available priests continues to decline. And so will the number of deacons serving Catholic parishes. But the sacramental nature of the church makes the priest's role as presider of the Eucharist essential for the spiritual vitality and ecclesial identity of the Catholic community. Maintaining or even expanding the number of ministers serving in parishes is no substitute for the alarming drop in priests available for parish ministry.

Acknowledging the courage and commitment of priests and pastoral ministers, what can the present situation tell us about the shape of pastoral ministry in the years ahead?

Father O'Malley's Successors

Older Catholics remember Bing Crosby playing the role of Fr. Chuck O'Malley in *Going My Way* and *The Bells of St. Mary's*. Crosby's Father O'Malley found a secure place in the Catholic imagination of the qualities and style of the ideal parish priest. Ministry, today's senior Catholics instinctively understood, was what happy, charming, and somewhat mysterious priests did.

There certainly were some priest ogres giving the lie to the idealized and romanticized Father O'Malley, but in general priests were genuinely admired and respected. The same admiration and respect were extended to the sisters who staffed the parish school. Although some features of this bygone era of parish life can still be seen, the overall face of parochial ministry at the turn of the century is considerably different.

Consider the following realities. It is estimated that about half the world's parishes are led by lay leaders. In the United States, studies reveal that approximately 80 percent of parish ministers are lay and that 80 percent of these are women.[4] Bishops, some still optimistic that the vocation crisis is over, continue to assign two or more parishes to the care of a single pastor while a growing number of women, mostly religious, are named parish administrators. In the rural diocese of New Ulm, Minnesota, covering almost 10,000 square miles and numbering almost 71,000 Catholics plus a migrant population of 10,000 men, women, and children, the deployment of pastoral personnel hints at what is likely to be common for most U.S. dioceses in the years ahead. Only forty-four of the diocese's eighty parishes have a resident pastor. Of the thirty-six parishes without a resident pastor, seventeen are administered by priests, sixteen by women religious, and three by laypersons.[5] With only forty-nine active diocesan priests to meet the pastoral needs of eighty parishes, a large number are assigned to more than one parish.

In southern California, the Archdiocese of Los Angeles' four million plus Catholics worship in 287 different parishes served by 418 active diocesan priests where Sunday Mass is celebrated in more than fifty different languages. Here, where 808 nonordained parish ministers outnumber active diocesan priests two to one, forty-one parishes are without a resident pastor.[6] The pastoral challenges facing dioceses as different as New Ulm and Los Angeles continue to grow as researchers report a 75 percent drop in seminarians, 40 percent drop in the number of priests, and a 50 percent increase in the Catholic population since 1950.

In Europe, the situation is even bleaker. Between 30 to 50 percent of parishes are without a resident priest. The vocation picture is as stark as it is in North America with the average age of priests approaching seventy.[7] In England, for example, Sr. Mellitus Lawlor is accustomed to showing visitors around the church and rectory of St. David's parish near Heathrow airport. Much more than a tour guide, Sister Mellitus runs the parish herself assisted by parish volunteers.[8] Her role at St. David's may soon be the norm for more than half of the world's parishes if the current ministry crisis is not forthrightly addressed.[9]

The sharp decline in the number of seminarians, the aging of Catholic clergy, and the growing population of Catholics are dramatically changing the face of parish ministry. As more and more religious, deacons, and lay ministers assume parish leadership roles, parishioners will witness a significant decline in opportunities for eucharistic worship. Priests simply will not be available for Mass. Somewhat bemused, Catholics will remember the voices of their pastors sternly reminding them that it was a serious sin to miss Mass on Sunday. Could this be, they will wonder, yet another failure in episcopal leadership?

The number of parish ministers may well hold steady, but the critical decline in the number of priests and resident pastors is threatening the very sacramental life of countless Catholics. Church authorities know this, but as we noted earlier, they urge only renewed recruiting efforts and evermore fervent prayers for vocations. This, I propose, is a failure in leadership.

Leadership

By the very nature of their office, bishops and priests assume leadership roles in the Christian community. From a theological perspective, they function as servant leaders, providing vision, inspiration, and direction to the faith community as well as pastoral and sacramental ministry.[10] Most bishops, priests, religious, and lay parochial ministers do their best to meet the pastoral needs of their parishioners. How well they meet their leadership responsibilities, however, is another matter.

Leadership from the Vatican

Arguably no other moral voice in the world has the stature and wields the clout of the papacy. Champion of social justice, national and international peace, the rights of the defenseless and the dispossessed, the papacy, especially during the long reign of John Paul II, has courageously and relentlessly stood as a beacon of moral conviction and life-giving hope to the citizens of the world. Whether critiquing the economic system of capitalism or condemning the materialistic culture of death, ethnic cleansing, or tribal genocide, the moral leadership of Pope John Paul has been undaunting.

Internally, on the other hand, the leadership of the Pope has been criticized—the strong centralization of church power in the Vatican and the procedure for appointing bishops with minimal or no consultation with conferences of bishops being two of the more neuralgic of his policies.[11] I will focus here, however, on an encyclical issued by Pope Paul VI in June 1967, *Priestly Celibacy (Sacerdotalis caelibatus)*. The encyclical is significant for its use and nonuse of New Testament citations in affirming mandatory celibacy for Latin rite priests.[12] In his important book, *Papal Sin*, Gary Wills notes a critical omission from the biblical citations relating to celibacy. His point is worth quoting at length:

> If you look at its *[Priestly Celibacy]* footnotes, you find a continual stream of citations from the New Testament. But only three places in the New Testament directly address the subject of this encyclical. Two of them are cited, not quoted, in a single footnote of the encyclical. The third, the most relevant, is nowhere even mentioned. The first two say this: "A bishop must be irreproachable, the husband of only one wife" (1 Tim 3:2), and "[a presbyter should be] a man unimpeachable, the husband of only one wife, with children of the faith" (Titus 1:7). . . .

But the third passage is the one that of itself should have precluded Paul VI's trying to write the encyclical in the first place. Saint Paul . . . is telling the Corinthians that he has not imposed on them—in fact, he has not even claimed all his rights "as an apostle." He says to them: "Have I not the right [*exousia*] to take a Christian wife about with me, like the rest of the apostles and the Lord's brothers, and Stone [Cephas]? . . ." But the point truly embarrassing to this argument is that word *exousia* (prerogative, or power). This is not a matter of permission or mere concession given to the apostles. It is a *right* that Paul possessed without exercising and Peter (Cephas) possessed and exercised—part of what Paul goes on to call "the right given me by my preaching" (1 Cor 9:18). If that was an apostolic prerogative, what right has anyone later to take away the right?[13]

Wills sees this omission as a significant example of the intellectual dishonesty he was chronicling in *Papal Sin*. It also serves as an example of the culture of denial addressed in these pages.[14]

If Andrew Greeley and others are correct, nothing so weakened the credibility and moral authority of the papacy, especially in matters of human sexuality, as Paul VI's 1968 encyclical *Humanae vitae*. Its many positive features were obscured by the Pope's decision to reject the recommendations of his own commission of highly qualified theologians, physicians, and lay leaders, in affirming an absolute ban on all forms of birth control save the rhythm method.[15] The experience of countless couples of the negative effects of the rhythm method on married love and spiritual intimacy was denied as well as the reasoned arguments of theologians, ethicists, and other church and scholarly authorities.

Moreover, the non-reception of *Humanae vitae* by the vast majority of married Catholic couples continues to be ignored—in effect, denied. Few bishops and pastors are heard today preaching against the widespread practice of birth control evident in many world cultures, especially in North America and Western Europe. It would be a healthy sign if the papacy acknowledged the non-reception of the 1968 encyclical and reflected on the lived experience of married Catholics. The faithful need to know that their experience is taken seriously by church authorities. There is, unfortunately, little evidence that Vatican authorities value the wisdom of God's people. A good number of bishops, I suspect, feel the same way. Either not consulted themselves by the various Vatican congregations or consulted in ways that reveal little real openness to their experience, they deal with their own frustrations as best they can.

Episcopal Leadership

In the years following Vatican II, United States episcopal leadership peaked in the 1980s with two prophetic pastoral letters from the National Conference of Catholic Bishops on peace and the economy—*The Challenge of Peace*, on nuclear war, and *Economic Justice for All*. While applauded widely by believers from many faith traditions for their prophetic courage, the bishops were criticized strongly by some U.S. military experts, journalists, and congressional leaders—the pastoral letter on the economy especially infuriated wealthy, conservative Catholic businessmen. The negative views, sometimes bitter and self-righteous, underscored the prophetic nature of the bishops' letters. In the eyes of their critics, however, the bishops were prophets without honor.

The listening, study, and consultation that shaped the bishops' pastorals remain models of postconciliar episcopal leadership. Sadly, criticism was also heard from the Vatican. Apparently, strong, national episcopal conferences are perceived as threats to the control deemed essential to the Vatican. In recent times, episcopal conferences have been drastically weakened by procedural guidelines from the Holy See, an abrupt turnaround from their strong affirmation following the council.[16]

Even when the U.S. bishops enjoy strong unanimity on issues that are properly theirs, for example, translations for lectionaries and sacramentaries and the implementation of *Ex corde ecclesiae*, the papal initiative requiring Catholic theologians to receive a *mandatum* (a license to teach from the local bishop)—to insure that Catholic institutions of higher learning are indeed Catholic—their authority has been eclipsed by the curial leaders of various Vatican congregations. As church historian Scott Appleby noted on national television in April 2002, the bishops now function as middle managers for the church's headquarters in Rome.[17] Even seasoned commentators on church affairs find it difficult to identify the leaders among the ideologically and theologically divided U.S. bishops.[18] Until they emerge, honest, fraternal communication and dialogue between the U.S. bishops and the bishop of Rome will be imperiled. Whether American bishops will soon be able to reclaim their proper authority as true shepherds of their local churches remains an important question for the church's vitality.

The Leadership of Priests

In times of crisis such as the church is facing in the first years of the twenty-first century—steep drops in the number of priests, an even more drastic decline in the number of vowed religious, and the tragic scandal of clergy abuse of minors—what keeps Catholics loyal to the church, they often report, is the leadership and ministry of their parish priest. If all politics are local, as former U.S. Congressman Tip O'Neill claimed, all vibrant church life is ultimately local, ultimately grounded in a local, worshiping community. There the priest, anointed by the Spirit, plays his critical role as preacher, teacher, pastor, and spiritual leader. If he does it well, the community of believers will survive the fiercest of crises. Where the priest is not a strong leader, the community often flounders. Without denigrating the pastoral care and leadership of lay and religious ministers, the growing number of parishes without resident pastors should be a critical concern for the church's national and international leaders.

Parishes with resident pastors, of course, observe different levels of gifts and competencies in their priests. Such has it always been and always will be. But regardless of their personal skills and talent for preaching, the present cloud of sexual abuse against teens and children hanging over the heads of priests makes leadership all the more difficult for the best of them. As more and more bishops feel a growing distance between the Vatican and their local diocese, more and more priests are beginning to feel that they are primarily filling slots on the personnel charts of their local chancery. Working harder than ever, with their ranks thinning annually, many experience a growing distance from their bishop and their brother priests. Some seem to have reduced their world to the boundaries of their parishes and simultaneously surrendered their responsibility to inspire and lead their parishioners. Leadership in times of crisis, they discover, demands considerable faith and courage.

If there is a crisis of leadership among the U.S. bishops, as I have suggested, there is a similar crisis of leadership in most diocesan presbyterates—the corps of priests in a given diocese. Sometimes as divided as their bishops over theological issues, pastoral concerns, and church polity, they forgo candid dialogue with their bishops, husbanding their energies for the demands of pastoral care. But the current crisis in episcopal leadership has left a vacuum in many dioceses that is proving intolerable to priests and laity alike. If my reading is correct, there are signs that leaders are emerging among the various U.S. presbyterates. From Boston to Chicago to Los Angeles, priests are drawing on untapped wells of courage to speak their truth to their confreres, their parishioners, and to their bishops, confident in the wisdom born of their pastoral experience, firm in their love of the church, and resolved to be both men of the church and their own men.

Lay Leadership

As the church's medieval clerical culture—a closed, male society of privilege, exemption, and deference—comes undone, the witness of lay leaders in the church is now emerging. Thoughtful, well-educated Catholic women and men are not only impatient with being treated like children, they are demanding to be heard as adults whose wisdom and life experience have, for too long, been dismissed. The age of the laity, evolving slowly since Vatican II, is now coming into its own, sparked by the unprecedented clergy abuse scandal ignited in Boston in January of 2002 discussed in chapter six. Their children were put at risk, and many were severely wounded by priest abusers, when nonmarried bishops and clerics alone determined what were reasonable risks for the young people of their dioceses. With their children wounded—many scarred for life and some taking their own lives—Catholic laity no longer tolerate being treated like children themselves. They seem to especially resent the "bad faith" concern of Vatican and local church authorities that they not be confused by honest discussion about the integrity and timeliness of certain church structures and disciplines.

When the Boston archdiocesan newspaper, *The Pilot*, published an editorial inviting discussion and review of mandatory celibacy, the cardinal archbishop expressed concern that the editorial "unfortunately created confusion." Arguably, the laity have never been less confused. And in the case of the sexual abuse scandal rocking the church in recent years, they speak with precision and insight. Anna Quindlen, for example, writes with passion and force in *Newsweek*:

> The bishops gathered wood for this current conflagration every time they turned away from the human condition to emphasize wayward genitalia. They must be amazed at how harshly they are now judged after all those years of deference, when they were allowed to make their own laws. Perhaps they sense that they are being judged with the ferocity of those accustomed to being judged harshly themselves. The judgment of divorced Catholics reborn in good marriages ordered not to go to communion. The judgment of women up all night with sick babies lectured about the sanctity of life. The judgment of hardworking, devoted priests who have watched the hierarchy cover up the dirt that sullies them, too. The judgment of now grown children who have taken to drink, drugs,

domestic violence, because of the shadow that Father's wandering hands have cast over their lives.[19]

Underneath their anger, they report, their love for the church of their ancestors remains constant, especially for the sacraments that nourish their souls and define them as Catholics. The laity, more than ever, as we have noted above, see their responsibility to minister to each other and to their priests. And if the bishops will let them, they will even minister to the prelates whose decisions betrayed their young.

In the present climate, lay leaders, married and single, parents and grandparents, are likely to speak up in dioceses from coast to coast with the passion and confidence of Anna Quindlen and others like her. Those with competence and wisdom, especially laity who have demonstrated leadership at the parish level, should be invited to a place at the chancery table. Their presence alone will lead to a more transparent church, to a healthier church, to a holier church.

As the laity assume more active roles in their parishes and dioceses, they will likely inspire in their priests and bishops a fresh understanding of the church as a communion of believers bound together by baptism and the renewing power of the Spirit. As theologian James Keenan writes:

> We are witnessing a sea change . . . in the relationship between pastors and laity. The way I explain this change is by comparing it to an earlier shift. Until the 1950s, nurses in the United States identified themselves primarily with the physician, but then shifted their advocacy role to the patient. Similarly, pastors, especially on the east coast, have often held a fealty to their local ordinary that supersede all other loyalties. Now, however, the pastor is more clearly defined by his responsiveness to his parish.[20]

The sea change of which Keenan writes has a corresponding effect on the laity's sense of responsibility for their church. Unshackled by the clerical culture controlling many priests and bishops, lay leaders will see through any attempts by clergy to put the image of the church and priesthood ahead of the well-being and safety of the faithful.[21]

Together with their bishops and pastors, lay leaders will begin to build a new household for the people of God—and a more open, accountable style of leadership. Rather than feared, their presence should be welcomed.

PART THREE
BEYOND DENIAL

CHAPTER TEN

SACRED SILENCE, SACRED SPEECH

To hold back information is to have power, and there is a "silence and listening . . . more useful than speech."

—Novelist Hilary Mantel, on writer John McGahern

Veritas odium parit, "Truth begets hatred."

—Latin proverb

The most serious problem facing us today in arriving at a more adequate understanding of the priesthood, theologically and practically, is a widespread inhibition of speech within the Catholic community.

—Robert J. Egan, *Commonweal*

MORE THAN A GENERATION HAS ELAPSED since the close of the Second Vatican Council. The tensions that simmered and sometimes erupted during its four-year duration continue to unsettle Catholics of every stripe. A step forward is taken and then followed by a step backward: Pope John Paul II beatifies the beloved John XXIII and then hastens to beatify the reactionary Pius IX.[1] We move cautiously toward Christian unity and then take a step back with claims that our sister churches aren't really sister churches after all. We affirm the role of the laity as gift of the Spirit and continue to exclude competent women and men from meaningful leadership roles in the church. We distinguish revealed truths from disciplinary customs and insist that even such practices as mandatory

157

celibacy for Latin rite priests may not be discussed. We deplore the victimization of our children by clergy and church personnel and exclude parents and adult victims from any meaningful role in shaping the policies put in place to deal with clergy abuse. We insist on the central role of the Eucharist and sacraments in the lives of believers and tolerate the absence of a resident priest in almost half of the world's parishes. We speak of transparency and accountability and maintain a feudal, clerical culture of secrecy. We solicit and accept contributions from parishioners and corporations and provide, at best, superficial financial reports. We speak authoritatively about human sexuality without listening to the lived experience of married, single, celibate, gay, and lesbian Catholics. We affirm our bishops as true shepherds of our local churches and treat them like branch managers. And perhaps saddest of all, we acclaim the equality and dignity of women and insist they maintain their distance—and their silence.

Due mainly to the crisis ignited by the John Geoghan scandal in January 2002, long simmering tensions are now at the boiling point—and close to overflowing. It is clear now that the tensions of the post-conciliar generation were but symptoms of a mounting anger in the hearts and souls of numerous Catholics. The scale and intensity of the anger—directed primarily at bishops and the church's culture of secrecy and control—suggests that the church will never be quite the same. We are, many believe, at the edge of a new epoch, an epoch cradled in both opportunity and danger. Never in the church's recent history has it been so in need of true sacred silence and true sacred, spirit-filled speech.

Sacred Silence

I write this final chapter in spring 2002 with the scandal triggered by the arrest and conviction of Boston priest John Geoghan still mounting. The scandal will get worse, much worse, say commentators who know the church well, before it will get better. In spite of this conviction which I share, and in spite of its dangers, I believe we are in the midst of a *kairos* moment, a moment distinct from chronological time because it is dense with the vibrancy of the Spirit. This graced time, like all *kairos* epiphanies, is pregnant with hope and possibility for a deeper experience of God's grace and saving power. Human freedom, however, is never eclipsed, not even in periods of history especially touched by the breath of the Holy One. How Christians and other people of faith respond to the present moment of grace in respectful silence, courageous speech, and wise action remains all important.

"It has already been pointed out," wrote Karl Rahner, "that the Christian of the future will be a mystic or he will not exist at all."[2] If Rahner's prediction proves prophetic, then today's Christian is challenged to bring a contemplative dimension to his or her life— not an easy task in societies driven by profit motives and fueled by fast-paced technologies. In such environments the very idea of sacred space and contemplative living seems anachronistic. Bringing a contemplative spirit to the office or community gathering simply doesn't compute, to use the techno-jargon of the day. Yet, the current crisis makes all the more urgent the need to be still, to quiet our souls, and to wait prayerfully—for a certain contemplative quiet is necessary for the voice of the Spirit to be heard.

Our church's contemplative tradition long ago discovered the wisdom and transforming power of mindfulness and awareness, of focused, prayerful attention. Rahner reminds us that a contemplative approach to living is the heritage of us all, and not restricted to monks and nuns behind cloister walls. It is, I'm convinced, the foundation of holy listening and holy speech and a vital component to a faith-filled response to the present *kairos* moment. Living contemplatively, I suggest, may well save our sanity in the spirit-crushing, fast-paced society in which we live. Such mindfulness or awareness, moreover, has the power to melt the fear and resentment that betray much of the current speech heard in church circles.

Only after prayerful, silent reflection can we hope to speak our truth in charity and with integrity and to act with wisdom and courage. Learning to sit quietly in the presence of God—even while waiting in checkout lines and traffic jams—will lead to needed reflection on the tensions and challenges currently facing the church. Without such moments of solitude and periods of thoughtful reflection, anger and resentment block the kind of open dialogue necessary for the church's vitality and health.

Social critic Morris Berman, in *The Twilight of American Culture*, places the hopes of what he sees as our unraveling culture on the "new monastic individual."[3] Berman refers here to the small number of people in every age and society who, as "new monks," live lives of such authenticity and wisdom that they preserve that which is true and noble in collapsing cultures like our own. According to Berman, these anonymous "monks," much like the Christian monks who preserved the learning of the classical period of civilization during the Dark Ages, are the only hope of a decaying culture. Like unrecognized contemplative elders, these secular "monks" model the kind of living that has healed the decaying cultures of the past and preserved what is true, noble, and good in them. Berman hopes they will heal and transform what he sees as our own present dark slide into chaos.

What we need now, I propose, are "new contemplative individuals" to point the way as the secrecy and control of the present clerical system comes undone. These men and women—laity, religious, priests, and bishops—will speak out of their silence and experience, out of their loyalty and commitment, and especially from what they have learned through nondefensive listening. When these "new contemplatives" speak there will be no denial, no half-truths, no minimization, no duplicitous spins. With courage and compassion they will point to invisible elephants and to emperors without clothes. They will generate, as the saying goes, more light than heat. From such contemplative voices, as we shall see shortly, a new direction, a new order, may emerge from the present darkness.

Sacred Speech

Aware of the dramatic impact the media has on the life and mission of the church, Vatican and diocesan officials are making efforts to deal more effectively with reporters, journalists, and commentators. An example of these efforts was a 2001 conference held in Rome for church communications officers on the subject of media relations. Archbishop Joseph Foley, president of the Pontifical Office for Social Communications, offered the following advice to the participants:

- First principle: Never, never, never tell a lie.
- Truth is not only morally right, it is politically correct and establishes an atmosphere of trust.
- Truth will always come out; failure to tell the truth is a scandal, a betrayal of trust, and a destroyer of credibility.
- Media often look for "weaknesses in institutions which preach virtue"; telling the truth opens space in media for good stories.
- So sacred is the responsibility to tell the truth that one must be ready to accept dismissal for refusal to tell a lie.[4]

Archbishop Foley's advice merits some comment. To his admonition to "never, never tell a lie," we might add that one should never tell a half-truth, never equivocate, never indulge in "corporate spins" that put institutional image ahead of the welfare of people, especially people without influence and power. Truth will indeed come out, but it may take years, even decades, for it to do so. During this meantime of obfuscation, innocent people, especially the young, may suffer needlessly. It is indeed a scandal for a church that proclaims to the world that it is the bearer of truth to fail to be truthful. It is likewise a scandal when church leaders fail to see the proverbial elephant in the room, when they fail to address issues that affect the spiritual well-being of Catholics—the forced fasting from Eucharist in many parts of the world being the most urgent.

Finally, Archbishop Foley insists: "So sacred is the responsibility to tell the truth that one must be ready to accept dismissal for refusal to tell a lie." Apparently church employees, from time to time, are asked to tell a lie "for the good of the church." Foley urges these individuals to forfeit their jobs if they are pressured by superiors or colleagues to be less than truthful—indeed a noble standard of professional and ethical behavior. Does not such a standard, it may be asked, apply equally to their ecclesial superiors—to the bishops for whom they work? The clergy sexual abuse scandals have laid bare actions on the part of some bishops that violate Archbishop Foley's admonitions. These bishops send abuser priests to other dioceses with letters testifying to their "good standing" and fail to inform pastors and laity when reassigning abuser priests to parishes within their own dioceses. For such bishops their credibility has been compromised, even shattered in some cases. When bishops are clearly culpable of failing to protect the safety of children and teenagers, Catholics wonder why they have turned a deaf ear to the forthright counsel of the president of the Pontifical Office for Social Communications.

Bearers of the Truth

The whole Christian community bears a responsibility to safeguard and to pass on the legacy of the gospel and its redeeming, liberating message.[5] It fulfills this duty when believers rooted in Christian community live out their lives according to the path shown to them by Jesus of Nazareth, whom they believe to be Jesus the Christ—the anointed Son of God. Should disciples of the Christ stray from the gospel's path, the bishops of the church in union with the bishop of Rome, serve as elders charged to safeguard the essence of the faith with divine assurance that the Spirit of God will keep them from egregious error. Such divine assurance has led over the centuries to a deep conviction that Christians, and here I refer to Catholic Christians, possess a revealed truth that surpasses all human knowledge. Until rather recent times this truth was often spoken of as the "deposit of faith," implying that it was somehow circumscribed, constant, and final. Bishops, and especially the pope, were its final, infallible arbiters.

The gift of faith that unites Christians in loving communion was, from the beginning, understood to be grounded in revealed truths, truths that, while never fully comprehended, could never be compromised. It is fidelity to the truths of faith—always formulated in historical context—that has made many church leaders especially wary of dialogue with the world, other faith traditions, and even within its own faith community.

Consider the approach to dialogue in the 1964 encyclical of Pope Paul VI, *Ecclesiam suam*. This is his first encyclical and it is remarkable both in tone and content. The Pope speaks humbly and pastorally about the nature and mission of the church to patriarchs, bishops, priests, laity, and indeed, "to all men of good will." The letter is divided into three sections titled *Awareness, Renewal, and Dialogue*. It is this last section on dialogue that is germane to our discussion. Early in Part 3, Paul writes, "The Gospel is light, it is newness, it is energy, it is rebirth, it is salvation"(59). No static notion here of a staid, impenetrable, legalistic monolith. Rather, the Pope points to the gospel as a dynamic, inviting, ever new invitation to live by the light of Christ's teaching and in the power of his spirit. This dynamic and pastoral tone permeates the entire encyclical.

Still, it is of interest to see how the letter understands the nature of dialogue from the church's perspective. Dialogue, it soon becomes evident, is welcomed by the church as an opportunity and occasion for evangelization and teaching: "The Church should enter into dialogue with the world in which it exists and labors. The Church has something to say; the Church has a message to deliver; the Church has a communication to offer"(65). And a few paragraphs later, Paul continues:

Did not our predecessors, especially Pope Pius XI and Pope Pius XII, leave us a magnificently rich patrimony of teaching which was conceived in the loving and enlightened attempt to join divine to human wisdom, not considered in the abstract, but rather expressed in the concrete language of modern man? And what is this apostolic endeavor if not a dialogue? (68).

The encyclical goes on to describe the characteristics that should accompany dialogue: clarity, meekness, trust, and pedagogical prudence (81). The underlying purpose of dialogue, however, remains evangelization. Church leaders and their delegates enter into dialogue to answer the questions of nonbelievers or believers of different faiths and to speak the truth of the gospel to all who would hear (81, #3). An honorable and even obligatory objective. What is not present, however, is any notion of mutuality, of both parties standing open to the possibility of being informed and even transformed as a result of the conversation. The closest the encyclical comes is to acknowledge that the church will discover elements of truth in the positions of her dialogue partner:

The dialectic of this exercise of thought and of patience will make us discover elements of truth also in the opinions of others, it will force us to express our teaching with great fairness, and it will reward us for the work of having explained it in accordance with the objectives of another or despite his slow assimilation of our teaching. The dialogue will make us wise; it will make us teachers (83).

Must the church, as bearer of the truth, the very word of God, always assume the posture of teacher and evangelizer? May it not remain bearer of the truth when it enters into dialogue with other churches—and even its own members—open to God's Spirit that may be heard from voices other than those of its hierarchy? I believe it may—and must. But it won't be easy. Alain Woodrow, writing in *The Tablet*, underscores why honest dialogue is so difficult for many church leaders:

If you are convinced that you possess absolute truth, doubt is inconceivable and pluralism out of the question. This logic led to the ancient claim of the Catholic Church, *Extra ecclesiam nulla salus* (no salvation outside the church) advanced with absolute authority.[6]

We have come a long way from the triumphalism captured in the banner cry of "no salvation outside the church." Catholics now may think of themselves as partners with all of humankind. Consider this striking paragraph from *Gaudium et spes* (Vatican II's Constitution on the Church in the Modern World):

> [A]s people who have been made partners in the paschal mystery, as people configured to the death of Christ, we will go forward, strengthened by hope, to the resurrection. *All this holds true not only for Christians but also for all women and men of good will in whose hearts grace works invisibly.* For since Christ died for all, and since all human beings are in fact called to one and the same destiny, which is divine, *we must hold that the Holy Spirit offers to all human beings the possibility of being made partners, in a way known to God alone, in the paschal mystery.* Such is the nature and greatness of the mystery of humankind . . . (GS 22, emphasis added).

In spite of our solidarity with the human family, in spite of being partners with all women and men of goodwill "in a way known to God alone," we remain suspicious of dialogue fearing that somehow our faith will be diluted. Unfortunately, dialogue for many in church leadership remains an opportunity not to be informed but, rather, to inform, instruct, and evangelize. While these objectives never can be foregone, they may be temporarily suspended so that the church might listen with an open heart to the God who speaks as she pleases, through whom she pleases.

The church may indeed have a "corner on the truth" thanks to the gospel she cherishes. It's clear, however, especially in light of the sexual abuse scandals of the last two decades, that she has no such corner on wisdom. It is time for a new order of sacred listening and sacred speech.

Fear of Dialogue

In his *America* essay, "How Bishops Talk," Bishop Kenneth Untener addressed the fear undergirding much of the silence and denial evident in the contemporary church.[7] He was prompted to write when Chicago's Cardinal Joseph Bernardin's 1996 "Catholic Common Ground Project" met with immediate and strong criticism from four U.S. cardinals—Cardinals Bernard Law, James Hickey, Adam Maida, and Anthony Bevilacqua. Bernardin's initiative for open dialogue and discussion on issues critical to the church disturbed his brother cardinals whose various responses are worth a brief examination.[8] Untener notes that:

> The [four cardinal] respondents seem to have confused dialogue with debate, arbitration, compromise, forging a consensus. The purpose of dialogue is clarity, not compromise. It is the basic, first step in trying to understand each other's position.
>
> The church always needs dialogue not only with those outside the church, but among its own members. In his major encyclical on the church *[Ecclesiam suam]*, Pope Paul VI uses the word "dialogue" 67 times. Each time, he uses it positively.[9]

In contrast, consider the following statements as quoted in Bishop Untener's *America* essay:

> Cardinal Law: "The fundamental flaw in this document [of Cardinal Bernardin] is its appeal for 'dialogue' as a path to 'common ground.' . . . Dissent from revealed truth of the authoritative teaching of the church cannot be 'dialogued' away. Truth and dissent from truth are not equal partners in ecclesial dialogue. . . . Dialogue as a way to mediate between the truth and dissent is mutual deception."

> Cardinal Hickey: "But we cannot achieve church unity by accommodating those who dissent from church teaching—whether on the left or on the right. To compromise the faith of the church is to forfeit our 'common ground' and to risk deeper polarization. . . . If the church is to be strong and convincing now and in the next millennium, it must preach the Gospel without compromise."

Cardinal Maida: "This statement [of Cardinal Bernardin] may create some confusion for people since it seems to suggest that Catholic teachings are open to dialogue and debate. . . . Dialogue is a helpful tool and step in a larger process, but of itself, it cannot solve religious differences."

Cardinal Bevilacqua: "[Catholic common ground] is an ordinary, everyday term, open to uncontrolled interpretation, including even the meaning that 'Catholic common ground' signifies 'lowest common denominator.' . . . A polite debate or a respectful exchange of divergent views about what would be the most commonly acceptable Catholic teaching is not sufficient to adequately address and heal the differences which exist among the faithful."

Nowhere, Bishop Untener points out, did the Common Ground statement talk at all about accommodation, compromise, or lowest common denominator. Each of the cardinals feared Bernardin's Common Ground initiative was somehow a threat to the faith, as their negative interpretation of dialogue makes clear. We are in trouble, I propose, when a U.S. church leader of Cardinal Bernardin's stature is perceived as a threat to the church's doctrinal integrity by extending an invitation to dialogue about pastoral and ecclesial concerns and issues. Even dialogue about doctrinal issues should not be discouraged since these sacred teachings remain open to ever fuller and deeper understandings.

Honest, Humble Dialogue

In *The Changing Face of the Priesthood,* I called for honest discussion about issues facing the priesthood and the church itself. I offered no solutions to the challenges facing the priesthood but rather urged that these challenges and issues be squarely addressed. It was my judgment that further silence and denial would seriously harm the health of the priesthood and the very vitality and mission of the church. Healthy discussion, I believe, would lead to the church's collective wisdom coming to the surface. New directions would sooner or later become clear as we faithfully listened to each other and to the Spirit. Discussion did follow, but it was informal and was never really encouraged by church authorities. The discussion, it should be noted, was accompanied by considerable controversy. Hailed in many corners for raising important concerns that were too long denied, *The Changing Face of the Priesthood* was roundly condemned in other corners of the church as disloyal and undermining of the priesthood. In spite of the controversy it ignited, the book nonetheless raised the prospect of a renewed and healthier priesthood—if only we could forthrightly address the issues and concerns at stake.

Can we imagine what the church would look like, what the priesthood would look like, if we entered into nondefensive, honest, and humble dialogue about the issues and concerns raised in Part Two of this book?

- We Catholics would affirm the sacramental nature of the church. If current church structures and disciplines were seen to be keeping believers from regular access to the sacraments, especially the Eucharist, we would change them. I believe the current imposed fasting from Eucharist in many parts of the world would be alleviated by a married priesthood in the Latin rite. Celibacy would be honored as a gift given to vowed religious, to some of the faithful and to some of the church's diocesan priests. The church would no longer claim that any candidate desiring to minister as a priest would *ipso facto* be a recipient of this gift. Priests who had left active ministry would be urged to discern whether God was calling them to some form of ministry, especially part-time sacramental ministry. Seminarians would be counseled to prayerfully determine, in dialogue with their spiritual directors and confidants, if they were blessed with the charism of celibacy.

- Women would be called to meaningful roles of leadership and ministry in the church including ordination to the diaconate. The theological and scriptural reasons put forward for denying women ordination to the priesthood would be reviewed in light of contemporary scholarship and gospel values. Women and men blessed with the charism of preaching would be called forth, trained where necessary, and commissioned to preach—even at the Eucharist. At present, a number of lay and religious women and men, holding doctorates in preaching, teach seminary courses in preaching while not being able to preach themselves, save at noneucharistic liturgies.

- Believers who practice their faith and publicly profess the creed of the church would no longer be required to take oaths of fidelity or make additional professions of faith before assuming church offices or before being called to the sacrament of orders. Attempts to enforce external compliance with doctrinal or ethical church teachings would be seen as contrary to the nature of faith and the role of conscience. The license or *mandatum* now required of Catholic scholars to teach theology in Catholic institutions of higher education would be lifted. Fidelity to the gospel and Catholic teaching would be assumed in the absence of evidence to the contrary. Moreover, theologians whose work is reported to the Congregation for the Doctrine of Faith as possibly erroneous or heretical would have the right to due process and to know the identities of their accusers.

- As a church, we would encourage experimenting with new forms of religious life, both apostolic and contemplative. Seminaries would be houses of formation situated on or near the campuses of Catholic colleges or graduate schools of theology; these institutions would

provide the academic component of seminary formation. Priests would be given the personal freedom to
choose their own residence and would receive salaries
that would allow them (with their families) to assume
responsibility for housing, food, and other living expenses. Clericalism would be challenged in an atmosphere of respect and support for all of the church's
ministers, lay and ordained.

- The church's theology of human sexuality would be
developed with an openness to the lived experiences of
men and women, married and single, straight and gay.
Bishops and other church leaders would reflect pastorally on the widespread non-reception of the
church's teaching on artificial birth control.[10] These
same church authorities would call for a renewed theology of marriage and a review of the present annulment procedures.

- Priests, religious, and laity would be involved in appropriate ways in the process for appointing bishops.
Diocesan bishops would make meaningful financial
reports to the local church and appoint competent lay
people, women and men, to leadership positions. The
veils of secrecy surrounding clergy and church personnel abuse of minors would continue to be lifted while
respecting and protecting the rights of victims to confi-
dentiality. Due diligence would be given to the possibility of false accusations and to the civil and canonical
rights of the accused. Review committees, including
parents and victims of clergy sexual abuse, would make
recommendations to the bishop on the possible return
to restricted forms of ministry of priest perpetrators.

Honest conversation, I am convinced, will unlock our imaginations and allow us, in fidelity to the gospel, to see new and fresh

structures of church life that will be grounded in the wisdom of God's Spirit. In such sacred conversations, the vision and hope of Vatican II may discover its "second wind."

Even as Catholics long for the potential of Vatican II to be more fully realized, dozens of bishops have signed a petition asking Pope John Paul II to convene a new ecumenical council. Among the signatories is Archbishop Stephen Hamao, head of the Pontifical Council for the Pastoral Care of Migrants and Immigrant People. In a May 2002 interview, Hamao remarked:

> I have attended many synods [special meetings of bishops] since 1983. I find that many of the themes and ideas are repetitive. Part of the problem is that a synod is only consultative, and cannot make decisions. It has been 40 years since Vatican II. I think it's time for another decision-making assembly. The world has changed. . . . Everything is still too Rome-centered.[11]

Hamao added that while the call for a new council might not be realistic, he believes it reflects "the voice of the people." Such a call is likely to go unheeded, especially in light of the failing health of John Paul II. But the next pope may hear the same request from far greater numbers. Among those signing the petition, it should be noted, is the retired archbishop of Sao Paulo, Brazil, Cardinal Paulo Evaristo Arns.

Conclusion

If the church is faithful to its prophetic calling, it will always be in trouble, for the gospel is indeed a subversive message.[12] The living Christ continues to comfort the afflicted and to afflict the comfortable. And while countless Christians, with the poor and powerless of the world, are close to despair as they long for comfort and deliverance, many others are more than comfortable and thus in need of challenge, in need of "affliction." And so, in this time of peril, the whole Christian world, including clergy and religious, is called to conversion of life, to listen anew to the voice that dares to speak for the hidden Christ in our midst. The voice of the church, we have seen, wounds and scandalizes when it does not "speak the truth in love." It fails its mission when it denies the reality of issues and concerns that affect the lives of its members. The trouble that marks every age of the church's history turns to peril, we have argued, when the church is less than candid, less than truthful. The lives of the more notorious medieval and Renaissance popes, cardinals, bishops, and lower clergy bear sad witness to the harm and evil that lies, deceptions, and equivocations have brought about. Much of our current pain can be traced to similar lies, denials, deceptions, and evasions. We should take little comfort that our current peril is not new, that it is as old as the "imperial church" whose origins are traced to the fourth century. For we, in this age, as in ages past, possess the abiding wisdom of the Spirit. It is time to draw on that wisdom and break the present, unholy silence.

Failure to engage in honest, unbridled, and respectful dialogue can only deepen the present crisis engulfing the church. Efforts to enforce silence or to limit speech, we should know by now, prove ineffectual and even counter-productive. The fear that motivates such efforts, I believe, reveals a lack of faith in Christ's promise that the Spirit would be with us—until the end of time. Some of us Christians, I fear, have come to put our faith in the institution rather than in the gospel it serves. To the extent that we have done so, we have committed small, invisible acts of petty idolatry that, like rushing water over rocks, have worn away the integrity and credibility of church leaders and the liberating power of Jesus' message.

Without healthy dialogue, the denial and "church spins" marking the first years of the present century will continue to threaten the integrity and credibility of our bishops and the very mission of the church. It is time to replace fear with confidence and control with trust. It is time for a holy silence and sacred listening. Above all, it is time for courageous, honest speech—a time to tell the truth in love.

NOTES

Introduction

1. Walter Brueggemann, *Deep Memory, Exuberant Hope* (Minneapolis: Fortress Press, 2000) 67.

2. Walter Brueggemann, *The Prophetic Imagination* (Philadelphia: Fortress Press, 1978) 49.

3. Ibid., 61.

4. Ephesians 4:15-16: "But speaking the truth in love, we must grow up in every way into him who is the head, into Christ, from whom the whole body, joined and knit together by every ligament with which it is equipped, as each part is working properly, promotes the body's growth in building itself up in love" (NRSV). See also Mary Catherine Hilkert, *Speaking with Authority: Catherine of Siena and the Voices of Women Today* (New York: Paulist Press, 2001).

5. See Rene Girard, *Violence and the Sacred*, trans. Patrick Gregory (Baltimore: Johns Hopkins University Press, 1979). Girard continues, "Far outranking these [tempests, forest fires, plagues, etc.], however, though in a far less obvious manner, stands human violence—violence seen as something exterior to man and henceforth as a part of all the other outside forces that threaten mankind. Violence is the heart and secret soul of the sacred," 31.

6. Ibid., 262.

Chapter One: Sacred Silence

1. See for numerous and tragic examples, Barbara Tuchman, *The March of Folly* (New York: Alfred A. Knopf, 1984).

2. See Eugene Kennedy, *The Unhealed Wound* (New York: St. Martin's Press, 2001). Kennedy offers a probing and relentless analysis of the present crisis of authority gripping the church. Also Donald Cozzens, "Telling the Truth," *The Tablet* (August 5, 2000) 1044–45, and "Facing the Crisis in the Priesthood," *America* (November 4, 2000) 7–10.

3. See Mary Catherine Hilkert, *Speaking with Authority: Catherine of Siena and the Voices of Women Today* (New York: Paulist Press, 2001) for a sustained reflection on the power of speaking the truth in love, especially ch. 2.

4. Austin Flannery, general ed., *Vatican Council II* (Northport, N.Y.: Costello Publishing, 1988) *The Church (Lumen gentium)*. "By reason of the

knowledge, competence or pre-eminence which they have the laity are empowered—indeed sometimes obliged—to manifest their opinion on those things which pertain to the good of the Church" (ch. IV, par. 37, 394).

5. Cited by Stephen Jay Gould, "What Only the Embryo Knows," *The New York Times* OP-ED (August 27, 2001).

6. See *Congregations* (March–April 2001) for an enlightened discussion on the pressures facing pastoral ministers today with particular focus on the dramatic decline in the number of clergy under age thirty-five, especially David J. Wood, "The Conditions of the Call," 16–19.

7. See Kennedy, *The Unhealed Wound*, ch. 10, "The Varieties of Ecclesiastical Control."

8. Raymond Hedin, *Married to the Church* (Bloomington and Indianapolis: Indiana University Press, 1995) 258, n. 16.

9. See Gil Bailie, "The Vine and Branches Discourse: The Gospel's Psychological Apocalypse," *Contagion: Journal of Violence, Mimesis, and Culture*, vol. 4 (Spring 1996) 121–45. See also Joan Chittister, "Discipleship for a Priestly People in a Priestless Period," an address given at the First International Conference of Women's Ordination Groups, Dublin, Ireland, June 30, 2001.

10. Donald B. Cozzens, *The Changing Face of the Priesthood: A Reflection on the Priest's Crisis of Soul* (Collegeville: The Liturgical Press, 2000).

11. David McCullough, *John Adams* (New York: Simon and Schuster, 2001) 226.

12. See Catherine Mowry LaCugna, *God for Us* (New York: HarperCollins, 1991). "The saints," she writes, "are those who have been converted by the gospel, *who live in conformity with the truth of their own personhood*, whose exercise of sexuality is a blessing, who are detached from wealth, whose words build up not denigrate others, who devote themselves to the service of others" (italics added), 409.

13. Cozzens, *The Changing Face of the Priesthood*, 19–20.

14. See Harry Levinson's "Why the Behemoths Fell: Psychological Roots of Corporate Failure," *American Psychologist*, vol. 49, no. 5 (May 1994) 428–36.

15. "Conscious Business: An Interview with Fred Kofman," *Sounds True* (Catalogue) no. 1, 5, 2002.

16. Ibid.

Chapter Two: Forms of Denial

1. For a comprehensive analysis of denial in its many faces, see Steven Cohen, *States of Denial: Knowing about Atrocities and Suffering* (Cambridge, England: Polity Press, 2001) 5.

2. Jean-Paul Sartre, *Being and Nothingness* (New York: Philosophical Li-

brary, 1956) 49. See also Joseph S. Catalano, *A Commentary of Jean-Paul Sartre's "Being and Nothingness"* (New York: Harper Torchbooks, 1974) 78–91.

3. See Michael Crosby's discussion of codependency as "external referencing," in *Celibacy: Means of Control or Mandate of the Heart?* (Notre Dame, Ind.: Ave Maria Press, 1996) 123–25.

4. Gary Wills, *Papal Sin: Structures of Deceit* (New York: Doubleday, 2000). It is, of course, unusual to hear of parents apologizing to their children, teachers to their students, managers to their employees, elected officials to the electorate.

5. See Wills, *Papal Sin: Structures of Deceit*, especially Part I, Historical Dishonesties, 11–69. See also Barbara W. Tuchman, *The March of Folly* (New York: Alfred A. Knopf, 1984) for numerous examples of historical denial, and Donald B. Cozzens, *The Changing Face of the Priesthood: A Reflection on the Priest's Crisis of Soul* (Collegeville: The Liturgical Press, 2000) 92.

6. Augustine, trans. by Henry Chadwick, *Confessions* 8.7.16 (Oxford, U.K.: Oxford University Press, 1991) 144.

7. See Michael Crosby, *The Dysfunctional Church: Addiction and Codependence in the Family of Catholicism* (Notre Dame, Ind.: Ave Maria Press, 1991).

8. David France, "Confessions of a Fallen Priest," *Newsweek* (April 1, 2002) 54.

Chapter Three: Sacred Oaths, Sacred Promises

1. Pius X, *Sacrorum antistitum* (September 1, 1910).

2. Marvin R. O'Connell, *The Harpercollins Encyclopedia of Catholicism*, Richard P. McBrien, general ed. (New York: Harpercollins, 1995) 926. Lawrence Barmann observes that *Pascendi dominici gregis* created both *modernism* and *modernists* since there was no defined or loosely defined movement espousing a common goal or declaring a common *manifesto*. "Obviously this is not to deny that, in an era when theological pluralism in both methodology and concept was unthinkable to Church authorities, many individuals in every western European nation and elsewhere were rethinking the great questions of Christianity, i.e., the meaning of revelation, the bible, Jesus Christ, the Church, and so forth, with methods and in terms and conceptions drawn from their own contemporary culture and outside of the authoritarian scholastic orthodoxy of Roman manual theology and canon law. What it does deny is that this was an organized movement of rebellion as Pascendi would have it, nor were the individuals involved destructive-minded persons out to ruin the Church as, again, Pascendi argues." See Lawrence Barmann, "The Modernist as Mystic: Baron Friedrich von Hugel," *Journal for the History of Modern Theology*, 4. Bd., S. (1997) 221–50. For an overview of the anti-Modernist era, see Gabriel Daly's *Transcendence and Immanence: A Study of Catholic Modernism and Integralism* (Clarendon: Oxford, 1980). For a comprehensive review of oaths commonly used in judicial church proceedings, see

Eugene Moriarity, *Oaths in Ecclesiastical Courts: An historical synopsis and commentary* (Washington, D.C.: The Catholic University of America, 1937).

3. John Tracy Ellis, "John Tracy Ellis: Church Historian," in Tim Unsworth, *The Last Priests in America* (New York: Crossroad, 1991) 84.

4. Ibid., 85.

5. Kilian McDonnell, "Spirit and Experience in Bernard of Clairvaux," *Theological Studies*, vol. 58 (1997) 3.

6. *American Catholic Quarterly Review*, vol. 35 (1910) 723–24.

7. *Presbyterorum ordinis*, in Austin Flannery, *Vatican Council II* (Northport, N.Y.: Costello Publishing, 1988).

8. John Tracy Ellis observes, "The seminary was seen as another West Point or Annapolis. There were frequent analogies drawn from the military." Ellis follows with this telling remark, "Here at Catholic University [where he taught church history], we had to take the oath against Modernism every year. The fact that we took it once wasn't enough. If you missed the ceremony, then you had to go to the office of the vice rector who would administer it the next day." Unsworth, *The Last Priests in America*, 85.

9. Cardinal Montini, archbishop of Milan (later Pope Paul VI), wrote the following *votum* to the Antepreparatory Commission for Vatican II: "One ought to consider seriously whether the provision for the swearing of an oath ought to be abolished, according to the statement in the gospel (Mt. 5:36), by substituting for it some word of the clear and honest profession of a sincere spirit" as quoted in *Report of the Catholic Theological Society of America, Committee on the Profession of Faith and the Oath of Fidelity* (April 15, 1990) 24. A generation earlier, in December 1939, another oath was rescinded with the approval of Pius XII, the oath against the Chinese Rites. Benedict XIV's constitution *Ex quo singulari* of 1742 condemned various rituals associated with the cult of Confucius and the veneration of ancestors which were presented to church authorities in Western theological categories that suggested they were superstitious. To emphasize the force of his degree, Benedict declared, "We want this Constitution of Ours to remain in force, all of it lasting for all time to come." See Peter C. Phan, "This Too Shall Pass," *Commonweal* (December 21, 2001) 13–15.

10. For a careful analysis of the theological and canonical issues related to the Profession of Faith and the Oath of Fidelity, see Michael J. Buckley, Margaret Farley, John T. Ford, Walter Principe, and James H. Provost, *Report of the Catholic Theological Society of America, Committee on the Profession of Faith and the Oath of Fidelity* (April 15, 1990).

11. Ladislas Örsy, *The Profession of Faith and the Oath of Fidelity: A Theological and Canonical Analysis* (Wilmington, Del.: Michael Glazier, 1990) 62, n. 30.

12. Profession of Faith, *Acta apostolicae sedis* (59, 1967, 1058).

13. Örsy, *The Profession of Faith and the Oath of Fidelity*, 35.

14. Harold M. Hyman, *To Try Men's Souls: Loyalty Tests in American History* (Berkeley: University of California Press, 1959).

15. CTSA, *Committee on the Profession of Faith and the Oath of Fidelity*, 15.

16. Ibid., "Henry A. Poels, professor of Scripture at The Catholic University, refused to sign an oath professing belief in the Biblical Commission's decree concerning the Mosaic authorship of the Pentateuch, and his contract was not renewed," 32. Margaret Mary Reher, *Catholic Intellectual Life in America* (New York: Macmillan, 1989), adds, "Beyond the personal pain suffered by Poels, the hierarchy's insistence that he sign the oath virtually wiped out scripture scholarship in the United States for several decades," 97.

17. Ibid., 8.

18. The church's long-standing concept of "reception" highlights the role the people of God, the faithful, play by receiving or accepting a church teaching or practice.

19. Margaret A. Farley, *Personal Commitments: Beginning, Keeping, Changing* (San Francisco: Harper and Row, 1986) 10.

20. Bernard Haring, *The Virtues of an Authentic Life: A Celebration of Spiritual Maturity*, trans. Peter Heinegg (Liguori, Mo.: Liguori Publications, 1997) 158–59.

Chapter Four: Voices of Women

1. Dolores Leckey, "Crossing the Bridge: Women in the Church," *Church* (Winter 2001) 11.

2. Ibid.

3. See John Paul II, *Mulieres dignitatem* (On the Dignity and Vocation of Women) *Origins* 18 (October 6, 1988).

4. See Arthur Jones, "Entrusting God's Word to the Entire Church," *National Catholic Reporter* (November 23, 2001) 12–13.

5. Bishops who held such sessions include Joseph Imesch, Rembert Weakland, and Raymond Lucker.

6. Jones, "Entrusting God's Word to the Entire Church," 16.

7. Ibid.

8. Quoted in Leckey, "Crossing the Bridge: Women in the Church," 16.

9. P. Francis Murphy, "Let's Start Over: A Bishop Appraises the Pastoral on Women," *Commonweal* (September 25, 1992) 12.

10. For further discussion on the need for skilled listening within the church, see Donald Cozzens, "Facing the Crisis in the Priesthood," *America* (November 4, 2000) 7–10.

11. In November 2001, the Vatican affirmed its teaching excluding women from ordination to the diaconate.

12. Walter Brueggemann, *Deep Memory, Exhuberant Hope* (Minneapolis: Fortress Press, 2000) 59.

13. Ibid.

14. Ibid., 59–60.

15. See Elizabeth A. Johnson, *She Who Is* (New York: Continuum, 1992) and *Friends of God and Prophets* (New York: Continuum, 1998). See also Mary Catherine Hilkert, *Naming Grace: Preaching and the Sacramental Imagination* (New York: Continuum, 1997) and especially *Speaking with Authority: Catherine of Siena and the Voices of Women Today* (Mahwah, N.J.: Paulist Press, 2001).

16. Hilkert, *Speaking with Authority*.

17. Brueggemann, *Deep Memory, Exhuberant Hope*, 61.

18. Catherine Mowry LaCugna, "Introduction," in Catherine Mowry LaCugna, ed., *Freeing Theology: The Essentials of Theology in Feminist Perspective* (New York: HarperSanFrancisco, 1993).

19. Ibid., 2.

20. See Elisabeth Schüssler Fiorenza, *In Memory of Her: A Feminist Theological Reconstruction of Christian Origins* (New York: Crossroad, 1983).

21. LaCugna, *Freeing Theology*, 2. LaCugna continues, "Christian feminism is a far-reaching critique of the fundamental sexism of the Christian tradition inasmuch as it has valued men over women, has seen masculine experience as normative for women's experience, has imaged God in predominantly masculine metaphors, or has used the Christian message to support violence against women." See also Sandra M. Schneiders, *Beyond Patching: Faith and Feminism in the Catholic Church* (Mahwah, N.J.: Paulist Press, 1991). "The question, in its starkest terms, is whether or not the Bible teaches the maleness of God and the inferiority of women. In other words, is patriarchy divinely revealed and therefore divinely sanctioned?" 37. Since I am not treating explicitly the realities of patriarchy and sexism in this chapter on the voices of women, it is helpful to quote Schneiders on both of these terms. "*Patriarchy* is the term that refers to the ideology and social system of 'father rule,' which was the virtually universal pattern of social organization in the world of the Bible. The biblical text pervasively reflects this domination-subordination pattern in human relations and often legitimates it as divinely ordained. Religiously legitimated or sacralized patriarchy is called *hierarchy*. Not only did the Catholic church not repudiate or condemn patriarchy in general, but it also taught that hierarchy was willed by Jesus as the only appropriate form of organization for the church. The legitimation of patriarchy in family and society follows logically from this theological premise. . . . The attitudinal and behavioral consequences of androcentrism and patriarchy is [sic] called, collectively, *sexism*, that is, the conviction, and its consequences in every sphere of life, that men are superior to women simply because they are male. In its more virulent forms sexism betrays its roots in *misogyny*, fear and hatred of women. The innumerable forms of discrimination,

marginalization, exclusion, oppression, and abuse of women and their dependents is sexism in action, often fueled by misogyny." "The Bible and Feminism," in LaCugna, *Freeing Theology,* 34–35.

22. John L. Allen, Jr., and Pamela Schaeffer, "Reports of Abuse: AIDS exacerbates sexual exploitation of nuns, reports allege," *National Catholic Reporter* (March 16, 2001).

23. Ibid.

24. Maura O'Donohue, "Personal Memo from Sr. Maura O'Donohue MMM: Meeting at SCR, Rome, 18 February, 1995," *National Catholic Reporter,* http://www.natcath.com, posted March 9, 2001. To my knowledge, no such visitator has been appointed.

25. *NCR* (December 7, 2001).

26. Concern for the faithful ministry of most missionaries is found in the following statement: "MISNA, a Rome-based missionary news service," according to the *National Catholic Reporter,* "said that while the instances of sexual abuse 'cannot and must not be denied or justified,' they represent 'marginal phenomenon' in comparison to the 'arduous and courageous work' of many missionaries, often in situations of great hardship." *NCR Staff,* "Vatican Says It Knows Nuns Are Abused" (March 30, 2001).

27. *The Tablet* (March 24, 2001) 403.

28. Ibid.

29. Charles Muchinshi Chilindda, "Africans Say Continent is 'Easy Prey,'" *National Catholic Reporter* (April 6, 2001).

Chapter Five: Religious Life and the Priesthood

1. See Sandra M. Schneiders, *New Wineskins: Re-Imagining Religious Life Today* (New York/Mahwah, N.J.: Paulist Press, 1986).

2. Sandra M. Schneiders, *Finding the Treasure: Locating Catholic Religious Life in a New Ecclesial and Cultural Context,* Religious Life in a New Millennium, vol. 1 (New York/Mahwah, N.J.: Paulist Press, 2000) and *Selling All: Commitment, Consecrated Celibacy, Community in Catholic Religious Life,* Religious Life in a New Millennium, vol. 2 (New York/Mahwah, N.J.: Paulist Press, 2001); vol. 3 is forthcoming.

3. Charles R. Morris, *American Catholic: The Saints and Sinners Who Built America's Most Powerful Church* (New York: Times Books, 1997) 179–80.

4. Other actresses capturing the mystique of the Catholic sister include Jennifer Jones in the *Song of Bernadette* (1943), Ingrid Bergman in *The Bells of St. Mary's* (1945), and Audrey Hepburn in *The Nun's Story* (1959).

5. Morris, *American Catholic,* 180.

6. Ibid., 318.

7. Ibid.

8. See Mary Gordon, "Women of God," *The Atlantic Monthly* (January 2002) 57–91.

9. See Schneiders, op. cit., n. 1 and n. 2

10. Morris, op. cit., 318.

11. U.S. Bureau of Census, Current Population Reports, P20–515 "Household and Family Characteristics: March 1998."

12. The birth rate is even lower in Europe. Consider the following sampling covering the period from 1965 to 1991: Italy, 1.27; Spain, 1.28; Portugal, 1.50; Austria, 1.50; France, 1.77; Poland, 2.06; Ireland, 2.18. Jan Kerkhofs, ed. *Europe Without Priests?* (London: SCM Press, 1995) 9.

13. Austin Flannery, *Vatican II, Gaudium et spes,* ch. 1, "The Dignity of Marriage and the Family." Reflecting on this chapter, Sandra Schneiders writes, "By abandoning the Tridentine claim (cf. Denzinger 1810) of the intrinsic superiority of consecrated celibacy to matrimony and emphasizing that 'consecration' and sending into the world in imitation of Jesus is foundational to ordained, lay, and Religious mission, the Council implicitly recognized the equality of diverse vocations in the Church," *Finding the Treasure,* 403–04, n. 8.

14. For an analysis of the nature and causes of the cultural decline threatening western culture, see Morris Berman, *The Twilight of American Culture* (New York: W. W. Norton & Co., 2000).

15. See Lawrence Cada and Raymond Fitz, *Shaping the Coming Age of Religious Life* (New York: Seabury Press, 1979) especially ch. 2, "The Life Cycle of a Religious Community." The authors write, "From a historical perspective, . . . a reasonable expectation would seem to be that most religious communities in the Church today will eventually become extinct," 59.

16. See James D. Whitehead, "Priestliness: A Crisis of Belonging," in *Being a Priest Today* (Collegeville: The Liturgical Press, 1992).

17. See Thomas F. O'Meara, *Theology of Ministry,* 2nd ed. (New York/Mahwah, N.J.: Paulist Press, 2000) and Louise Bond, "Jubilee 2000: Celebrating Lay Ecclesial Ministry," *Sisters Today* (November 2000) vol. 72, no. 6, 402–09.

18. National Center for Pastoral Life's 1997 study as reported in Bond, ibid., 403–04. An editorial in the January 11, 2002, *National Catholic Reporter,* reported that "[a] May 2000 survey found that the average parish had grown 23 percent in the preceding 15 years, while the number of priests serving those parishes had declined 28 percent. . . . Currently some 30,000 Catholics are employed at least 20 hours a week in ministries associated largely with parishes. Another 35,500 are enrolled in 314 training programs ranging from diocesan certification classes to graduate programs in seminaries and universities," 20.

19. "The Lay Alternative to Closing Parishes," *National Catholic Reporter* (January 11, 2002) 20.

20. See Richard A. Schoenherr and Lawrence A. Young, *Full Pews and Empty Altars: Demographics of the Priest Shortage in United States Catholic Dioceses* (Madison: University of Wisconsin Press, 1993). "The Roman Catholic Church faces a staggering loss of diocesan priests in the United States as it moves into the 21st century. There is little chance of reversing this trend in the lifetime of the current generation of Churchgoers," xvii. See also Joseph Claude Harris, "The Shrinking Supply of Priests," *America* (November 4, 2000) 16–17, and "Supply, Demand and Parish Staffing," *America* (April 10, 1999) 16–20. The staggering drop in the number of U.S. priests is similar to the sharp decline in Europe. See Jan Kerkhofs' important study, *Europe Without Priests*, trans. John Bowden (London: SCM Press, 1995).

21. As the number of active diocesan priests in the U.S. drops below the 20,000 figure, the number of resigned priests well exceeds 20,000!

22. Donald B. Cozzens, *The Changing Face of the Priesthood* (Collegeville: The Liturgical Press, 2000) 132.

23. Hillary Wicai, "Clergy by the Numbers," *Congregation* (March–April 2001) 6–9. It should be noted that most mainline Protestant churches are also concerned with the number of their clergy aged thirty-five and under.

24. Dean R. Hoge, *The First Five Years of the Priesthood: A Study of Newly Ordained Catholic Priests* (Collegeville: The Liturgical Press, 2002). See also David Briggs, "Isolated Life Takes Toll on New Priests," *The Cleveland Plain Dealer* (October 19, 2001) A 1.

25. James E. Sullivan, "Don't Give the Priest Shortage the Silent Treatment," *U.S. Catholic* (December 2001) 26.

26. Katarina Schuth, *Seminaries, Theologates, and the Future of Church Ministry* (Collegeville: The Liturgical Press, 1999) 58. Schuth gives a balanced, realistic view of the present state of U.S. seminaries and theologates including profiles on the kind of seminarians preparing for the priesthood.

27. See Wicai, op. cit., and Schuth, op. cit.

28. See Cozzens, *The Changing Face of the Priesthood*, ch. 7, "Considering Orientation."

29. Paul Philibert, "Issues for a Theology of Priesthood: A Status Report," in Donald J. Goergen and Ann Garrido, eds., *The Theology of Priesthood* (Collegeville: The Liturgical Press, 2000) 1.

30. Sullivan, "Don't Give the Priest Shortage the Silent Treatment," 26.

31. Ibid., 27.

32. Ibid.

33. See Kenneth Woodward, *Making Saints* (New York: Simon & Schuster, 1990). Woodward writes, "The Church has placed a higher value on virginity than on marriage, even though marriage has the status of a sacrament while virginity does not."

34. Claire Schaeffer-Duffy, "Models of Holiness and Married Life," *National Catholic Reporter* (December 28, 2001) 5. Theologian William P. Roberts, quoted in Schaeffer-Duffy's essay, observes, "I don't know of any [married couples] who were canonized because of their marriage. There has always been a bias against marriage. The holiness of marriage, the goodness of sexual intimacy has never been officially recognized as a call to sanctity. Although the pope has made a lot of good statements with regard to marriage, in practice, the bias is still there," ibid., 5.

35. Thomas Merton, *Dialogues with Silence: Prayers and Drawings*, Jonathon Montaldo, ed. (San Francisco: HarperSanFrancisco, 2001) vii.

36. Sandra Schneiders notes the problem with the distinctions *apostolic* and *contemplative, active* and *enclosed* as well as the term *monastic*, op. cit., 303, n. 2. See Morris Berman's *Twilight of American Culture* (New York: W. W. Norton & Co., 2000) for a fascinating treatment of what he calls the *New Monastic Individual* (NMI). Berman places his hope for a renewed American culture in individuals committed to lives of learning and to the best of Enlightenment values.

37. The perils of perfectionism are captured in the poem "Perfection, Perfection":

I have had it with perfection.
I have packed my bags,
I am out of here.
Gone.

As certain as rain
will make you wet,
perfection will do you in.
It droppeth not as dew
upon the summer grass
to give liberty and green
joy.

Perfection straineth out
the quality of mercy,
withers rapture at its
birth.

Before the battle is half begun,
cold probity thinks
it can't be won, concedes the
war.

I've handed in my notice,
given back my keys,
signed my severance check, I
quit.

Hints I could have taken:
Even the perfect chiseled form of
Michelangelo's radiant David
squints,
the Venus de Milo
has no arms,
the Liberty Bell is
cracked.

Kilian McDonnell, *Adam on the Lam: The Uses of Impertinence* (Waite Park, Minn.: Park Press, 2000) 2, 3.

38. Mary Gordon, "Women of God," *Atlantic Monthly* (January 2002) 58. The caption introducing Gordon's article reads, "Nuns are an endangered species. With a median age in this country of sixty-nine, and little new blood coming in, their numbers have dwindled markedly. The novelist and memoirist Mary Gordon . . . examines this disappearing way of life, talks to survivors here and abroad, and wonders what, if anything, can replace the iconic figure of the nun in the popular imagination of Catholics and non-Catholics alike."

39. See Schneiders, *Finding the Treasure*, especially chs. 7 and 8.

40. Schneiders, *Finding the Treasure*, 110.

41. For a fuller discussion of the vocation crisis in terms of Catholic culture, see Cozzens, *The Changing Face of the Priesthood,* 132–35.

42. Walter Truett Anderson, *Reality Isn't What It Used to Be* (San Francisco: HarperSanFrancisco, 1990) 3. See also Paul Lakeland, *Postmodernity: Christian Identity in a Fragmented Age* (Minneapolis: Fortress Press, 1997).

43. Berman, *The Twilight of American Culture,* 168.

44. Robert Schreiter, "Major Currents of Our Times: What They Mean for the Church," *Origins* (August 16, 2001) vol. 31, no. 11, 195.

45. See Sandra Schneiders insightful treatment of religious life in a postmodern context in *Finding the Treasure*, ch. 3, 99–119.

46. In addition to the comprehensive and penetrating analysis of Sandra Schneiders cited above, n. 2, see Mary Jo Leddy, *Reweaving Religious Life: Beyond the Liberal Model* (Mystic, Conn.: Twenty-Third Publications, 1990) and Patricia Wittberg, *The Rise and Fall of Catholic Religious Orders: A Social Movement Perspective* (Albany: State University of New York Press, 1994).

Chapter Six: Abuse of Our Children

1. Msgr. Patrick O'Shea of the Archdiocese of San Francisco has been held in the city's Hall of Justice since April 2000. Charged with more than two hundred counts of child molestation, his bail was set at $5 million. See Stephanie Salter,

"Good Priests Pay Price of Church's Denial," *San Francisco Examiner* (February 19, 2002) A 11.

2. See Eugene Kennedy, *The Unhealed Wound: The Church and Human Sexuality* (New York: St. Martin's Press, 2001). Kennedy provides a penetrating analysis of the clerical world's conflicted, ambiguous understanding of human sexuality—and its tragic consequences.

3. See Donald B. Cozzens, *The Changing Face of the Priesthood: A Reflection on the Priest's Crisis on Soul* (Collegeville: The Liturgical Press, 2000) ch. 8, "Betraying Our Young," 111–25.

4. A. Richard Sipe, "The Problem of Prevention in Clergy Sexual Abuse," in *Bless Me Father for I Have Sinned* (Westport, Conn.: Praeger, 1999) 114–21.

5. Ibid., 115.

6. John Thavis, Catholic News Service reported in the *National Catholic Reporter* (February 8, 2002) 5.

7. Sipe, "The Problem of Prevention in Clergy Sexual Abuse," 115.

8. Clifford Longley, "The Right to the Truth," *The Tablet* (November 3, 2001) 1554.

9. Sipe, "The Problem of Prevention in Clergy Sexual Abuse," 116.

10. Ibid., 117.

11. The 1962 British film *Lolita* features the seductive behavior of a pubescent girl.

12. Rod Dreher, "Sins of the Fathers," *The National Review* (February 11, 2002) 28. Dreher is quoting Msgr. Robert Rehkemper, former vicar general for the diocese.

13. Sipe, "The Problem of Prevention in Clergy Sexual Abuse," 119–21.

14. John Cornwell, *Breaking Faith: The Pope, the People, and the Fate of Catholicism* (New York: Viking Compass, 2001) 146–47.

15. Ellis Hanson, *Decadence and Catholicism* (Cambridge, Mass.: Harvard University Press, 1997) 297.

16. See Douglas E. Dandurand, *Implications of Mandated Celibacy for the Psychospiritual Development of Roman Catholic Clergy: A Qualitative Inquiry,* doctoral dissertation, Institute of Transpersonal Psychology (Palo Alto, Calif.: 2001) especially the self-report of "Phil," describing his attraction to postpubescent boys, 218–30. Dandurand's work deserves careful study by church officials and seminary personnel.

17. Rod Dreher quotes a priest who met with the family of a child who had been abused by one of the diocese's priests. "When we sat down face to face with them and the lawyers, we told them that the bishop had said his first priority was to do the right thing. We told them our investigation had found that the priest was guilty, but that he had never been in this kind of situation before. We had removed him from any further parish involvement. We told them that we didn't believe we had been neglectful, but we wanted to help the family in any way we

could, because we recognized lives had been damaged, and we were profoundly sorry. . . . I looked across the table, and the family was crying. The father said, 'Thank you. We never want to persecute anybody. That was all we wanted to hear.'" *National Review* (February 11, 2002) 30.

18. Michael Paulson, "After Sex Abuse Scandals, Many Priests Tread Warily," *The Boston Globe* (January 13, 2002) A 1.

19. Paulson, op. cit., A 1. One editorial cartoon labeled "Catholic Church Cover-up," depicts "a goofy-looking man in a miter and cardinal's robe. He holds a leash that is attached to the spike-studded collar of a huge, ferocious dog that has just taken bites out of the rear ends of two little kids in T-shirts and shorts. The cardinal tells the kids, 'It's nothing to worry about. After all, he wears the collar. . . .'" Salter, op. cit.

20. John L. Allen, Jr., "Vatican Moves to Address Sex Abuse Problem," *National Catholic Reporter* (December 7, 2001) 5.

21. Derrick Z. Jackson, *The Boston Globe* (February 13, 2002) A 23.

22. Joseph Claude Harris, "The Church Is Not Broke," *America* (April 5, 1997) 18.

23. "In Landmark Deal, Catholic Church Agrees to Payout in Sex-abuse Cases," Associated Press (January 31, 2002).

24. John L. Allen, Jr., "Doctrinal Congregation Given Authority Over Sex Abuse Cases," *National Catholic Reporter* (December 14, 2001).

25. See Michael H. Crosby, *Celibacy: Means of Control or Mandate of the Heart?* (Notre Dame, Ind.: Ave Maria Press, 1996) and Douglas E. Dandurand's doctoral dissertation, *Implications of Mandated Celibacy*.

26. Lisa Miller, David France, "Sins of the Fathers," *Newsweek* cover story (March 4, 2002). Reporting on the Boston archdiocese's handling of the Geoghan case and featuring the stories of some of the victims, the writers note: "Pedophilia, which researchers admit they know little about, is believed to afflict 5 to 6 percent of all men (and hardly any women). Of these, most never act on these impulses. After a sex scandal in the early 1990s, the Chicago archdiocese opened up records for all 2,252 priests who served there over a period of 40 years. Only one of the priests had allegedly assaulted a preteen. The most common complaints involved boys who were 15 or 16," 45–46. A review of other media stories of clergy abuse will substantiate this reality. See Andrew Greeley, "How Serious Is the Problem of Sexual Abuse by Clergy?" *America* (March 20–27, 1993) 6–10.

27. See Cozzens, *The Changing Face of the Priesthood*, 124.

28. Pam Belluck of *The New York Times*, reporting on Judge Sandra Hamlin's sentencing of John Geoghan, wrote, "The judge said Mr. Geoghan, a small puckish-looking man who chatted with his sister and chuckled during much of the trial, showed 'a total lack of concern for the damage his sexual molestation may have done.'" "Ex-Priest in an Abuse Case Is Sentenced to 9 to 10 Years," *The New York Times* (February 22, 2002) A 16.

29. Elsewhere I proposed that these members of the clergy were "focused sociopaths." Cozzens, *The Changing Face of the Priesthood*, ch. 8, "Betraying Our Young," 123.

30. Andrew Sullivan, "They Still Don't Get It," *Time* (March 4, 2002) 10.

31. Cozzens, *The Changing Face of the Priesthood*, ch. 8, "Betraying Our Young," 125.

32. Greeley, op. cit., 6–10. Greeley, it should be noted, does not see a connection between celibacy and the sexual abuse of minors.

33. Johanna McGeary, "Can the Church be Saved?" *Time* (April 1, 2002) 31.

34. See the U.S. bishops' "Charter for the Protection of Children and Young People" and their norms for dealing with accusations of sexual abuse of minors by church personnel adopted at their June 13–15, 2002, meeting in Dallas. *New York Times*, June 15, 2002, A 10.

35. Dandurand, *Implications of Mandated Celibacy*, 281.

36. As quoted in Sipe, "The Problem of Prevention in Clergy Sexual Abuse," 121.

37. John Geoghan, accused of molesting more than 130 children over a thirty-year period, was sentenced on February 21, 2002, to a maximum sentence of nine to ten years for fondling a ten-year-old boy in a swimming pool. *The New York Times* (February 22, 2002) A 16.

38. Michael Newton, "Father James Porter: Pedophile Priest," www.crime library.com/serial11/porter/ and Rod Dreher, op. cit., 27.

39. "Cardinal Says Scandal Won't Force Him Out," *The New York Times*, (February 11, 2002) A 21.

40. William F. Buckley, Jr., "Lawlessness in Boston," *National Review Online*, posted February 12, 2002.

41. Lisa Gentes, Catholic News Service, "Cardinal Apologizes to Abuse Victims, Says He Will Not Resign" (January 28, 2002).

Chapter Seven: Clerical Culture

1. *The Journals of Father Alexander Schmemann, 1973–1983* (Crestwood, N.Y.: St. Vladimir's Seminary Press, 2000) 311.

2. While heard less often today, it was common then to hear people refer to clergy as "the good fathers" and to nuns as "the good sisters." A cheery, "How'ya doing, Father?" was followed up with "That'a boy, Father!"

3. See Donald B. Cozzens, *The Changing Face of the Priesthood: A Reflection on the Priest's Crisis of Soul* (Collegeville: The Liturgical Press, 2000) ch. 1, "Discovering an Identity," 3–13, for a fuller discussion of the evolving identity of the priest.

4. James D. Whitehead, "Priestliness: A Crisis of Belonging," in *Being a Priest Today* (Collegeville: The Liturgical Press, 1992) 22–23. See also Michael L.

Papesh, "Farewell to the 'Club,'" *America* (May 13, 2002) 7–11, and Donald J. Goergen and Ann Garrido, eds., *The Theology of Priesthood* (Collegeville: The Liturgical Press, 2000).

5. Mark Jordan describes the difficult to define term "camp" by citing four of its more prominent features: irony, aestheticism, theatricality, and sharp humor. "In applying 'camp' to clerical culture, we should reconceive it as a series of effects rather than as a set of conscious motives. We have to understand irony and sharp humor as products of situations or systems, with or without the conscious consent of those acting in them. Aestheticism and theatricality can be present underneath their explicit denial, just as they can exist alongside bad taste and ugly mediocrity. Clerical camp is produced not by deliberate parody with caustic intent, but by a set of roles and styles that present themselves as perfectly 'normal.'" *The Silence of Sodom: Homosexuality in Modern Catholicism* (Chicago: The University of Chicago Press, 2000) 181–82. Ch. 7, "Clerical Camp," 179–208, is particularly relevant to our discussion. Jordan continues, "The expectations we impose on the Catholic priest, especially the combination of celibacy and ritual, bend his public gender—make him 'queer' in several senses. We then specify that the priest be officially homophobic. This makes his gender-bending on odd and bitter camp. Because that role is just what we have been taught to assign to priests, we don't speak of it as camp. We no longer recognize its queerness, in part because we wouldn't know what a 'straight' clerical culture would look like," 186. For a treatment of dandyism in the priesthood, see Ellis Hanson, *Decadence and Catholicism* (Cambridge, Mass.: Harvard University Press, 1997) 241–63.

6. James F. Garneau, "More Priestly Fraternity," *America* (October 22, 2001) 12. My read of such gatherings is far less benevolent than the author's. Furthermore, my experience in seminary formation is strikingly different from Garneau's. Papal encyclicals and Vatican and episcopal documents as well as the classic theological sources, St. Thomas Aquinas in particular, are very much a part of most seminary curricula. Katarina Schuth has responded to Garneau's academic assertions and his read on priestly culture in "Different Findings," *America* (November 12, 2001) 44.

7. *In Solidarity and Service: Reflections on the Problem of Clericalism in the Church* (Washington, D.C.: Conference of Major Superiors of Men, 1983) 2.

8. Ibid., "Persons other than clerics can exhibit the traits of clericalism. Lay people, religious men and women are liable to the pitfalls of clericalism in certain situations. Generally speaking, exclusive, elitist or dominating behavior can be engaged in by any person or group within the church. Such behavior is properly termed clericalism when it rests on a claim to special religious expertise or ecclesial authority, based on role or status in the church."

9. See Mary Collins, "The Refusal of Women in Clerical Circles," in *Women in the Church* (Washington, D.C.: The Pastoral Press, 1987) 51–63.

10. "Bishops Selection Process Blasted," *National Catholic Reporter* (October 19, 2001) 5.

11. Thomas Cahill, *Pope John XXIII* (New York: Viking, 2002) 19–20.

12. Ibid., 5.

13. See Cozzens, *The Changing Face of the Priesthood*, ch. 4, "Facing the Unconscious," and ch. 5, "Becoming a Man."

Chapter Eight: Gay Men in the Priesthood

1. See Donald B. Cozzens, *The Changing Face of the Priesthood* (Collegeville: The Liturgical Press, 2000) especially ch. 7, "Considering Orientation," 97–110.

2. Mark Jordan, *The Silence of Sodom: Homosexuality in Modern Catholicism* (Chicago: The University of Chicago Press, 2000) 106.

3. Ibid., 107.

4. Rod Dreher, "Sins of the Fathers," *National Review* (February 11, 2002) 30.

5. Ibid. For a fuller treatment of clerical networking, see A. W. Richard Sipe, *Sex, Priests, and Power: Anatomy of a Crisis* (New York: Brunner/Mazel, 1995) 174–75.

6. Ibid., Dreher.

7. Ibid., Dreher.

8. Brad Gooch, "Abbey Road," *Out* (April 2002) 46.

9. Ibid., 47.

10. Mark Jordan, *The Silence of Sodom* (Chicago: The University of Chicago Press, 2000); James Alison, *Faith Beyond Resentment: Fragments Catholic and Gay* (New York: Crossroad, 2001); Ellis Hanson, *Decadence and Catholicism* (Cambridge, Mass.: Harvard University Press, 1997).

11. Ibid., 110. Concerning seminary admissions committees, Jordan believes, "Gay men are assigned to implement policies designed to screen out or cure gayness. . . . Seminary admission decisions are occasions not only for acts of survival, of cultural reproduction, but of cultural repetition. Seminaries are and have been finishing schools for a certain kind of homoerotic identity. Efforts to weed out gay candidates, to cure them or teach them concealment, repeat the oldest conditions for producing homoerotic identity in Christian Europe. A Catholic seminary, especially a conservative seminary, is one of the few places left in modern society for building baroque closets. This is not so much the work of the effeminate candidate as it is of homoerotic clerical cultures trying to compete against the ideals of 'coming out.' Seminary education is often enough training in how to be homoerotic the old-fashioned way," 160–61.

12. Op. cit., 101–02.

13. William McDonough, "Acknowledging the Gift of Gay Priestly Celibacy," *Review for Religious*, vol. 55, no. 3 (May–June 1996) 283–96.

14. Judy L. Thomas, "Concern Grows Over AIDS Rate Among Priests," *The Kansas City Star* (November 5, 2000) A 25.

15. Ibid., A 1.

16. See Rob Dreher, *National Review*, and the recent books on the gaying of the Jesuits and the priesthood.

17. See Joe Fitzgerald's essay in the *Boston Herald*; see also Dreher above.

18. Richard P. McBrien, "Homosexuality and the Priesthood: Questions We Can't Keep in the Closet," *Commonweal* (June 19, 1987) 380–83; Andrew M. Greeley, *National Catholic Reporter* (November 10, 1989) 13.

19. Francis X. Clines, "Scandals in the Church," *The New York Times* (April 27, 2002) A 14.

20. John D'Arcy, *South Bend Tribune* (April 7, 2002).

21. Gary Wills, "The Scourge of Celibacy," *The Boston Globe* (March 24, 2002).

Chapter Nine: Ministry and Leadership

1. Johanna McGeary, "Can the Church Be Saved? *Time* (April 1, 2002) 28–40. "[S]ome dioceses adopted hardball legal tactics that abused victims all over again. . . . Church lawyers attack the victims' credibility and besmirch their families. They bombard victims with as many as 500 written questions, demand 30 years' worth of tax returns, require names and dates for every doctor visited back to age 12. They cross-examine mothers about their children's sex lives," 34. See also Angie Cannon and Jeffery L. Scheler, "Catholics in Crisis," *U.S. News & World Report* (April 1, 2002) and David France, "Confessions of a Fallen Priest," *Newsweek* (April 1, 2002).

2. See Lisa Sowle Cahill, "A Crisis of Clergy, Not of Faith," *The New York Times* (March 6, 2002) A 21. Cahill's essay is a powerful example of lay leadership in the church. Lay Catholic theologians, especially theologians who are parents, are demonstrating true leadership in their teaching and writing.

3. Reinhold Stecher, "Challenge to the Church," *The Tablet* (December 20–27, 1997) 1668.

4. "Frequently Requested Church Statistics," www.georgetown.edu/research/cara.

5. *The Official Catholic Directory, 2001* (New Providence, N.J.: P. J. Kenedy & Son).

6. Ibid.

7. See John Cornwell, *Breaking Faith: The Pope, the People, and the Fate of Catholicism* (New York: Viking Compass, 2001) 149–52.

8. Annabel Miller, "No Priest, No Problem," *The Tablet* (August 25, 2001) 1201–02.

9. In the last decades of the twentieth century, England and Wales suffered a 45 percent drop in vocations, with similar sharp declines on the Continent.

10. See Robert M. Schwartz, *Servant Leaders of the People of God* (New York: Paulist Press, 1989). See also his "Servant of the Servants of God: A Pastor's Spirituality," in *The Spirituality of the Diocesan Priest* (Collegeville: The Liturgical Press, 1997) 1–19.

11. See Cornwell, *Breaking Faith: The Pope, the People, and the Fate of Catholicism*, ch. 15, "Hierarchy."

12. I am indebted here to Gary Wills for his treatment of the New Testament sources quoted in Paul VI's encyclical. See his *Papal Sin: Structures of Deceit* (New York: Doubleday, 2000) ch. 8, "The Pope's Eunuchs," especially 122–27.

13. Ibid., 125.

14. See the dubious but anecdotally interesting *Shroud of Secrecy: The Story of Corruption within the Vatican* by Monsignor Luigi Marinelli and The Millenari, a group of anonymous Vatican prelates (Milan, Italy: Kaos edizioni Milano, 1999), English trans. by Ian Martin (Toronto: Key Porter Books Limited, 2000). "Kaos Editions originally released 7,000 copies of *Via col vento Vaticano* [*Shroud of Secrecy*]. When, in June 1999, Vatican officials issued an order to cease publication and distribution, sales soared to more than 100,000 copies. Sales continued to climb as both the Italian and international press picked up the story. As this book went to press, more than 200,000 copies of *Via col vento in Vaticano* were in print, and foreign editions were in high demand. *Shroud of Secrecy* is one such edition." Ed. note.

15. See Charles R. Morris, *American Catholic: The Saints and Sinner Who Built America's Most Powerful Church* (New York: Random House, 1997) 359–64.

16. See John L. Allen, Jr., *Cardinal Ratzinger: The Vatican's Enforcer of Faith* (New York: Continuum, 2000) 61–64.

17. ABC Special Report with Peter Jennings, *The Sins of the Fathers: The Church in Crisis* (April 3, 2002).

18. Certainly there are articulate and courageous leaders in the U.S. body of bishops. But to this date there has not been the necessary critical mass of bishops willing to stand publicly with them.

19. Anna Quindlen, "Patent Leather, Impure Thoughts," The Last Word, *Newsweek* (April 1, 2002) 74.

20. James Keenan, "The Purge of Boston," *The Tablet* (March 30, 2002) 18.

21. See Robert Kiely, "We Must All Save the Church," *The Tablet* (March 9, 2002). Kiely writes, "Among all the many victims of the Boston scandal are the ordinary parishioners and priests who struggle every day to keep their faith

communities together while around them churches close and the shortage of trained, valued and encouraged religious educators, counsellors, and ministers grows more acute. These are not simply problems for bishops and church officials; they are problems for all the People of God. When we are reminded that the Church is not a democracy, we need to remind the reminders that the Church is also not supposed to be a dictatorship: that its basis is love, and that love implies equality before God, 'neither slave nor free, neither Greek nor Jew, but Christ is all in all,'" 6.

Chapter Ten: Sacred Silence, Sacred Speech

1. "*La tradizione son' io! La chiesa son' io!*" (*I* am the Tradition! *I* am the Church!) screamed Pius IX to Cardinal Guidi. Quoted in Thomas Cahill, *Pope John XXIII* (New York: Viking, 2002) 70.

2. Karl Rahner *Concern for the Church, Theological Studies XX,* trans. Edward Quinn (New York: Crossroad, 1998) 149. Rahner continues, "If by mysticism we mean, not singular parapsychological phenomena, but a genuine experience of God emerging from the very heart of our existence, this statement is very true and its truth and importance will become still clearer in the spirituality of the future."

3. See Morris Berman, *The Twilight of American Culture* (New York: W. W. Norton, 2000) 135–36.

4. *Crux of the News* (newsletter) April 30, 2001.

5. "We think it is a duty today for the Church to deepen the awareness that she must have of herself, of the treasure of truth of which she is heir and custodian and of her mission in the world," Pope Paul VI, *Ecclesiam suam* (1964) no. 18.

6. Alain Woodrow, "Fascists for God," *The Tablet* (November 10, 2001) 1590.

7. Kenneth E. Untener, "How Bishops Talk," *America* (October 19, 1996) 9–15.

8. "Called to Be Catholic: Church in a Time of Peril," *America* (August 31, 1996) 5–8.

9. Untener, op. cit., 12.

10. "Called to Be Catholic," *America* (August 31, 1996). The Common Ground document includes the statement, "[A]n essential element of Catholic leadership must be wide and serious consultation, especially of those most affected by church policies under examination. The church's ancient concept of reception reminds us that all the faithful are called to a role in grasping a truth or incorporating a decision or practice into the church's life," 8.

11. John L. Allen, Jr., "31 Bishops Sign Petition for New Council," *National Catholic Reporter* (May 10, 2002) 7.

12. See Walter Brueggemann, *Deep Memory, Exuberant Hope* (Minneapolis: Fortress Press, 2000) ch. 1, "Preaching as Sub-Version," 1–18.

INDEX

abuse, understanding the meaning of, 104
accountability, 29–30
to hierarchical institutions, 29
Acton, Lord, 140
Adams, Abigail, 19
African sisters, abuse of, 60–61
Agre, Cardinal Bernard, 120
AIDS, 60, 62
denial of by hierarchy, 130–31
Alison, James, 129
Allen, Jr., John L., 119, 120
altruism in discerning religious vocation, 81–82
ambition, clerical, 121–23
repressed, 123
Anderson, Walter Truett, on postmodern world, 86
anger of laity against church authorities, 6
annulment procedures, need for dialogue on, 170
Appleby, Scott, on ecclesial leadership, 150
approval and clerical ambition, 122
aptitude, as quality for religious vocation, 80–81
Arns, Cardinal Paulo Evaristo, 171
artificial birth control, need for dialogue on, 170
Augustine, St., 32, 43

bad faith, 27–28
Barmann, Lawrence, on *Pascendi dominici gregis*, 175 n. 2

Bells of St. Mary's, 144
Berman, Morris, on postmodern world, 86–87
on "new monastic individual," 160
Bernard of Clairvaux, 14
Bernardin, Cardinal Joseph, 166, 167
Bertone, Archbishop Tarcisio, 91, 136
Bevilacqua, Cardinal Anthony, 136, 166, 167
birth rate in Europe, 180 n. 12
bishops, and authority, 16
appointment of, 170
fear of changes in church, 18–20
responsibilities of, 17–18
Bollas, Christopher, 26
Boniface VIII, Pope, 112
Boston Archdiocese, sexual abuse scandal in, 133
Boston Globe, The, 98, 100, 132
Bowers, Bob, 98
boys most often abused by clergy, 102, 105
Brueggemann, Walter, 5, 7, 56, 57
Buckley, Jr., William F., 111

Cahill, Thomas, 119–20
Catherine of Siena, 11, 49
Catholic family, downsizing of, 69–70
Catholic moral system and human sexuality, 108
celibacy, and morale of priests, 77
as a gift, 169
in hierarchy of dignity, 78–79
mandatory, 102, 103, 108
Challenge of Peace, The, 149

change, resistance to, 13
Changing Face of the Priesthood, The,
    18, 19, 77, 124, 126, 129, 167, 168
children, sexual abuse of, 89–90
church as pilgrim people, 25
    as promise of salvation, 25
church's resistance to change, 13
Clarke, Maura, 143
clergy abuse of minors, 27
    adolescent minors, 132
    extent of, 97
    factors that define, 105–06
    implications of, 96–97
    meaning of, 93
    profile of, 138
clergy sexual abuse scandal, 5–6
clergy sexual misconduct, denial of, 126
clerical ambition, 121–23
clerical culture, 114–15
    negative aspects of, 115–16
clerical system, weaknesses of, 139
clericalism, 117–19
closeted homosexuality, 129
Cohen, Steven, 26–27
Common Ground initiative, 166–67,
    191 n. 10
common vocation, 78, 79
compassion and sensitivity, need for,
    129
conceit of clergy, 38–39
Congar, Yves, 14
conscience, conflict regarding
    Modernism oath, 39–41
    fidelity to, 45–46
    manifestation of, 108
conscience formation in clergy
    abusers, 105
consumerist society, 70
contemplative spirit, need for, 159
contextualization, 30
convent culture, collapse of, 67–71

conversion of life, call for, 171
Conway, Neil, 33
Copernicus, 14
Cornwell, John, 94–95, 96
Corral Mantilla, Bishop Victor, 120
Courage, failed, 28
cowardice as moral act, 25
crisis, signs of, 56
Crosby, Bing, 144
cultural transition, 85–88

D'Arcy, Bishop John, 136
Dandurand, Douglas, on mandatory
    celibacy, 108
decline in priest population, 145
denial, 11, 17, 26, 51, 140–41, 105
    among victims of abuse, 33
    faces of, 91–94
    historical, 31–32
    and loyalty to authority, 28–29
    parallels in corporation and church,
        22
    personal, 32–34
    of priest shortage, 142–43
    presumptive, 30–31
    reasons for, 62
    of vocation crisis, 75–76
"deposit of faith," 163
diaconate, permanent, 72–74
    training for, 74
dialogue, need for, 170
    on annulment procedures, 170
    appointment of bishops, 170
    artificial birth control, 170
    celibacy as a gift, 168
    financial reports, 170
    lay leadership, 170
    lay preaching, 169
    mandatum required of Catholic
        scholars, 169
    married priesthood, 168

meaningful roles for women, 169
new forms of religious life, 169
oaths of fidelity, 169
priests' salaries, 170
review committees, 170
seminary formation, 169
theology of human sexuality, 170
veils of secrecy lifted, 170
dialogue, honest, 167–72
dialogue, in *Ecclesiam suam*, 163–66
Dinter, Paul E., 112
discipleship, call to, 78
disloyalty, 13
Dogmatic Constitution on Church,
  The, 14
Donovan, Jean, 143

Ecclesia in Oceania, 98–99
ecclesial transition, 7
Ecclesiam suam, 163, 166
Economic Justice for All, 149
ecumenical council, new, 171
Egan, Robert J., 124, 157
elitism, suspicious of, 82
Ellis, John Tracy, on oath against
  Modernism, 176 n. 8
  on *Pascendi dominici*, 38
emotional maturity, importance in
  priesthood, 102–03
Enlightenment, 86
entitlement, clerical attitude of, 116–17
ephebophilia, 133
episcopal clericalism, 119–20
episcopal conferences weakened by
  Vatican controls, 149
episcopal leadership, 149
Eucharist worship, decline in, 146
Ex corde ecclesiae, 44, 149–50
exaltation and humility, 83
exile experience, 7
existential guilt, 28

faithful as ministers of healing, 141–42
Fangman, Esther, 61
Farley, Margaret, 45
fear, 25, 58
fidelity, oath of, 41–42
financial reports, secrecy of, 170
financial resources and clergy abuse
  scandal, 100–01
fiscal implications of clergy abuse of
  children, 99–102
Foley, Archbishop Joseph, on dealing
  with media, 161–62
Ford, Ita, 143

Galileo, 14, 17
Gaudium et spes, 165
Gautin, Cardinal Bernard, 122
gay Catholic clergy, 102, 105
  church's denial of, 128–29
  considered as objectively disordered,
    135–37
  dark side of, 137
  pain and conflict of, 135
  silence of, 125–26
  as scapegoats, 135
Geoghan, John J., 89, 99, 105, 110, 111,
  132, 158, 185 n. 28, 186 n. 36
Gethsemani, Abbey of, 128
Girard, Rene, 8, 173 n. 5
Going My Way, 144
Gooch, Brad, 127–28
Gordon, Mary, 83
Greeley, Andrew, 106, 134, 148
Gregory the Great, Pope St., 119

Hamao, Archbishop Stephen, 171
Hanson, Ellis, 95, 129, 132
hardball tactics in clergy abuse
  settlements, 141
Haring, Bernard, 46
Harris, Joseph Claude, 100

Heaven Knows, Mr. Allison, 68
Hedin, Raymond, 16
Hickey, Cardinal James, 166
hierarchical order, 29
historical denial, 31–32
Hoge, Dean, 75
homosexuals in the priesthood,
    124–34, 137
Hufgard, Kilian, 1
human experience, value of, 22, 45
human sexuality, free expression of,
    107
  judged as sinful outside of marriage,
    107
Humanae vitae, 46
  non-reception of, 148, 170, 191 n. 10

idealism in religious life, 82
imagination, crisis in, 57
  viewed with suspicion, 57–58
imagination, faithful, 56–59
imagining, new ways of, 57
Imesch, Bishop Joseph, on pastoral
    letter on women, 53–54
inferiors on hierarchical ladder, 28–29
institutional dynamics, 22–25
institutional instinct, 30

Joan of Arc, 14
John Chrysostom, 37, 43
John Paul II, Pope, 44, 79, 98–99, 147,
    157, 171
  and apologies, 30, 98
John XXIII, Pope, 58, 78, 157
Jordan, Mark, 125, 129, 132
  on "camp" as clerical culture,
    186–87 n. 5
  on seminary admission committees,
    188 n. 11
Judge, Mychal, 134
  heroism of, 144

Jung, C. G., 65

Kairos moment, 159
Kansas City Star, The, 130, 131
Kazel, Dorothy, 143
Keenan, James, on relationship
    between pastor and laity, 153
Kelty, Matthew, 124
Kennedy, Eugene, 89, 109
Kerr, Deborah, portrayal of idealized
    nun, 68
Kofman, Fred, on political/social
    chaos in Argentina, 23–24
Kos, Rudy, 93

L'Osservatore Romano, 76
LaCugna, Catherine Mowry, 58, 174
    n. 12
  on Christian feminism, 178 n. 21
Law, Cardinal Bernard, 91, 166
  and denial, 110, 111
Lawlor, Mellitus, as parish adminis-
    trator, 146
lay ecclesial ministry, 72–74
  growth of, 72
  in parish administration, 73
lay leadership, 151–54
  in parishes, 145
  need for dialogue about, 170
  women in, 145
lay ministry, growth of, 144
leadership, 146–49
  and religious vocation, 81
leadership, lay, brings fresh under-
    standing of church, 153
  intolerant of childlike treatment,
    152
  love for the church, 153
  sparked by clergy abuse scandal,
    151–54
leadership of priest, 150–51

crisis of, 151
as pastor, teacher, preacher, spiritual
    leader, 150
Leckey, Dolores, 50–51, 53
listening hearts, 54–55
Longley, Clifford, 92
Los Angeles archdiocese, demography,
    145
    shortage of priests, 145
loyalty, 12–15
    to authority, 28

Maida, Cardinal Adam, 166, 167
mandatory celibacy, 102, 103, 108
mandatum, 150, 169
Mantel, Hilary, 157
Marinelli, Monsignor Luigi, 190 n. 14
married priesthood, need for dialogue
    on, 168
Martinez, Cardinal Eduardo, 61
Mass attendance, decline in numbers,
    85
Mass stipends, 31
maturity, importance of, 102–03
McBrien, Richard, 134
McDonald, Marie, 61–63
McDonnell, Kilian, 38–39, 182–83 n. 37
McDonough, William, 130
McGeary, Johanna, 106
media, as enemy of the church, 92
    effective communication with, 161
Merton, Thomas, 79–80
minimization, 11, 17, 26, 30
    reasons for, 62
missionaries, Catholic, 101
Mitchum, Robert, 68
modern world, relationship with, 84–85
Modernism, 86
    oath against, 37–38, 39
    effects of oath against, 43–44
modernity's effect on church, 86

monies paid to abuse victims, 101
moral courage, 34
moral cowardice, 25, 28
Morris, Charles R., 69, 70
    on contributions of women religious,
    67–68
Mulcahy, Francis, of M*A*S*H*, 26
Murphy, Bishop P. Francis, 54–55
Murray, John Courtney, 14

National Catholic Reporter, 60, 61,
    63, 119
    abuse of women religious by clergy,
    60
Navarro-Valls, Joaquin, 61, 137
New Ulm diocese, demography, 145
    shortage of priests, 145
New York Review, The, 43
non-reception, ancient concept, 191
    n. 10
Humanae vitae, 148, 170

O'Donohue, Maura, 59–64
O'Meara, Thomas, 2, 72
O'Neill, Tip, 150
oath against Modernism, 39
    failure of, 43
oath of fidelity, 41–42
oaths, swearing of, 176 n. 9
original sin, 12
Örsy, Ladislas, 42

Papal Sin: Structures of Deceit, 30,
    147–48
parish ministers, women as, 51
parochial minister, 143
Pastoral Constitution on the Church
    in the Modern World, 84
pastoral implications of clergy abuse
    of children, 97–99

pastoral letter on women, failed, 53–55
pastoral ministry, 101
   future of 144–46
Paul VI, Pope, 7, 46, 147–48, 163, 164
   on Evangelization in the Modern
      World, 54
Paulson, Michael, on Geoghan scandal,
   98
pedophilia, 102, 133, 134, 185 n. 26
"Perfection, Perfection," poem by
   Kilian McDonnell, 182–83 n. 37
perpetrators of abuse as masters of
   denial, 33
personal denial, 32–34
Philibert, Paul, 76
Pilot, The (Boston archdiocesan
   newspaper), 110, 152
Pius IX, Pope, 157
Pius X, Pope, 37, 86
Pius XI, Pope, 164
Pius XII, Pope, 164
Porter, James, 91, 105
postmodernism, 86–88
   effects on religious vocations, 87
power and social status, 16–18
pre-conciliar caste, 116
presumptive denial, 30–31
priest demographics, 74–75
Priestly Celibacy, encyclical on, 147
priests, decline in numbers, 74–77,
   145
   morale of, 76
   professional courtesies given to, 113
   ratio of to Catholics, 74
   unearned respect afforded to, 113–14
profession of faith, 41
   required for ordination, 42
promises, fidelity to, 44–45
prophetic witness, religious set apart
   for, 84
prostitution, 93

Quattrocchi, Luigi and Maria, 79
Quindlen, Anna, 152–53

Rahner, Karl, 159
Ratzinger, Cardinal Joseph, 122
Reardon, Christopher, 110
Reicks, Laura, 69
religious life, need for restructuring, 67
religious vocations, decline in numbers,
   66–67
remorse, lack of, 105
resignation of priests, reasons for and
   percentages, 75
resistance to change, 13
responsibility, 15–18
Romero, Archbishop Oscar, 143
Ruether, Rosemary, 49

Sacerdotalis caelibatus, 147
sacred oaths, 48
   promises, 44–48
   silence, 158–60
   speech, 161–62
sacred, defined, 8
salaries of priests, 170
Sartre, Jean-Paul, 27
Schaetzing, Eberhard, on ecclesiogenic
   neurosis, 109
Schmemann, Alexander, 112, 114
Schneiders, Sandra M., 65, 85
   on hierarchy, 178 n. 21
   patriarchy, 178 n. 21
   religious life, 67
   religious in modern world, 85
   sexism, 178 n. 21
Schreiter, Robert, on postmodernity, 87
selected blindness, 29
Selik, Richard, on AIDS, 131
seminary admission committees, 188
   n. 11
   enrollment figures, 75

formation, need for dialogue, 169–70
sexual abuse of children, cases of, 90
sexual exploitation of women religious, 60–61
sexual orientation and abuse of children, 134
Shroud of Secrecy, 190 n. 14
silence, 11, 15
  breaking, 59–64
  of institutional church, 109
simony, 31
single-parent Catholic families, 85
Sipe, A. Richard, 33, 91, 92–93
  on manifestations of denial, 94
Stecher, Bishop Reinhold, 142–43
Steele, Diane, 69
straight subculture, 131–32
structural implications of clergy sexual abuse, 102–03
Suenens, Cardinal Joseph, 14
Sulivan, Jean, 11
Sullivan, Andrew, 106
Sullivan, James E., 76, 77

Tablet, The, on mandatory celibacy, 62, 63, 92
temperament, and religious vocation, 80
tensions in the church, 157–58
Teresa of Avila, 14
theology of human sexuality, need for dialogue on, 170
Thomas Aquinas, on use of oaths, 43
Thomas, Judy L., on AIDS among clergy, 130–31
titles as hallmarks of clericalism, 120
tranquility, 18–20
Truth, 12
  bearer of, 162–65
  common, 22

need for, 161–62
official, 20–22
shaped by human experiences, 20
Twilight of American Culture, 160

Untener, Bishop Kenneth, 166

Vatican Council II, 39, 86, 157
Vatican directives on clergy abuse, 107
Vatican, leadership from, 147–49
victims of abuse, boys as, 105
violence, human, 173 n. 5
virginity in hierarchy of dignity, 79–80
vocation crisis, 78–82
  denial of, 75–76
vocation, common, 78, 79
von Baer, Karl Ernst, 15

Walker, Bishop David, 119
Ward, Archbishop of Cardiff, 92
Whitehead, James D., 65, 115
Wills, Gary, 30, 139, 147–48
Wolf, Abbot Nokter, 60
women and ordination to diaconate, 55
women religious, 71
  decline in numbers, 71
  demographics of, 69
  dialogue with bishops, 55
  downsizing, 71–72
  facing reality, 71–72
  future of, 69
  sexual exploitation of, 60–61
women, faithful imagination of, 59
  increasing roles of, 50
  leadership roles of, 50–51
  to be taken seriously, 58–59
women's fidelity to the church, 51
Woodrow, Alain, 164–65

Ziemann, Bishop Patrick, 127

Praise for Donald Cozzens' award-winning and bestselling book, *The Changing Face of the Priesthood:*

". . . as comprehensive and honest an examination of conscience of the American priesthood as we have seen." *America*

"It is Cozzens' love for the priesthood that motivates the book. He speaks warmly of the majority of priests in whom he finds great hope." *National Catholic Reporter*

"He speaks with great love and affection for his Church and great concern for its future." Aaron Brown, ABC News

". . . a reasoned, calmly-written yet impassioned plea that the Church and the priesthood he so loves should face up to realities." Paul Wilkes, *The Tablet*

"This is the most important book on the priesthood I have read for many years. It is a breath of fresh air in that it is authentic, helpful, and open." Dean R. Hoge, Life Cycle Institute, The Catholic University of America

". . . artistically paints the very soul of the priesthood. The result is a masterpiece which captures its triumphs and tribulations, hopes and doubts, loves and disillusions, and the mysterious powers that sustain it." Rev. Eugene F. Hemrick Syndicated Columnist, Catholic News Service

"It is full of wisdom and insights, success and failure, hope buttressed by the inspiration of the Holy Spirit." Theodore M. Hesburgh, C.S.C., President Emeritus, University of Notre Dame

"The best thing that's been written on the current state of the Catholic priesthood in recent times." Sandra M. Schneiders, Jesuit School of Theology, Berkeley As quoted in *The Boston Globe*